Christ

D0719555

To David,

Wishing you many happy hours with
these poems.
        Love,
            Mum & Dad.

LATER COLLECTED VERSE

BOOK TWO

RHYMES FOR MY RAGS

CONTENTS

This edition published in Great Britain 1979
by Ernest Benn Limited
25 New Street Square, Fleet Street, London EC4A 3 JA
& Sovereign Way, Tonbridge, Kent, TN9 1RW

Copyright © 1954, 1956, 1965 by Dodd, Mead & Company, Inc.
Copyright © 1960 by Germaine Service

Printed in the United States of America

British Library Cataloguing in Publication Data

Service, Robert William
Later collected verse.
811'.5'2   PR6037.E72A17

ISBN 0-510-32404-5

LATER
COLLECTED
VERSE

BY ROBERT SERVICE

ERNEST BENN · LONDON

BOOK THREE

VERSE FROM PROSE WRITINGS

BOOK FOUR

SELECTIONS FROM
UNPUBLISHED VERSE

BOOK FIVE

COSMIC CAROLS

CAROLS OF AN
OLD CODGER

PRELUDE

They say that rhyme and rhythm are
Outmoded now.
I do not know, for I am far
From high of brow.
But if the twain you take away,
Since basely bred,
Proud Poetry, I dare to say,
Would scarce be read.

With humble heart I thus define
My rôle in rhyme:
Oh may I never write a line
That does not chime.
And though a verse be nigh as sweet
As honey-comb,
To please me, let it have the beat
Of metronome.

So to my modest muse I give
A grateful pen;
Of lowliness I sing, who live
With lowly men.
And though I never cease to grieve
Poetic lack,
I do my best,—please take or leave
A Verseman's Pack.

2

RHYMES FOR RIPENESS

PORTRAIT

Because life's passing show
    Is little to his mind,
There is a man I know,
    Indrawn from human kind.
His dearest friends are books;
    Yet oh how glad he talks
To birds and trees and brooks
    On lonely walks.

He takes the same still way
    By grove and hill and sea;
He lives that each new day
    May like the last one be.
He hates all kinds of change;
    His step is sure and slow:
Though life has little range
    He loves it so.

He makes it his one aim
    His pleasure to repeat;
To always do the same,
    Since sameness is so sweet;
In simple things to find
    The dearest to his mood.
His true life in the mind
    Is oh so good!

Please leave him to his dream,
  This old, unweary man,
Who shuns the busy stream
  And has outlived his span.
Just leave him on his shelf
  To watch the world go by . . .
Because he is—*myself:*
  Yea, such be I.

MY ROCKING-CHAIR

When I am old and worse for wear
I want to buy a rocking-chair,
And set it on a porch where shine
The stars of morning-glory vine;
With just beyond, a gleam of grass,
A shady street where people pass;
And some who come with time to spare,
To yarn beside my rocking-chair.

Then I will light my corn-cob pipe
And dose and dream and rarely gripe.
My morning paper on my knee
I won't allow to worry me.
For if I know the latest news
Is bad,—to read it I'll refuse,
Since I have always tried to see
The side of life that clicks with glee.

And looking back with days nigh done,
I feel I've had a heap of fun.
Of course I guess that more or less
It's you yourself make happiness
And if your needs are small and few,
Like me you may be happy too:
And end up with a hope, a prayer,
A chuckle in a rocking-chair.

EIGHTY NOT OUT

In the gay, gleamy morn I adore to go walking,
And oh what sweet people I meet on my way!
I hail them with joy for I love to be talking,
Although I have nothing important to say.
I cheer the old grannies whose needles are plying;
I watch the wee kiddies awhoop at their play:
When sunny the sky is, you'll not be denying
The morning's the bonniest bit of the day.

With hair that is silver the look should be smiling,
And lips that are ageful should surely be wise;
And so I go gaily with gentle beguiling,
Abiding for cheer in the bright of your eyes.
I look at the vines and the blossoms with loving;
I listen with glee to the thrush on the spray:
And so with a song in my heart I am proving
That life is more beautiful every day.

For I think that old age is the rapture of living,
And though I've had many a birthday of cheer,
Of all the delectable days of God's giving,
The best of the bunch is my eightieth year.
So I will go gay in the beam of the morning
Another decade,—Oh I haven't a doubt!
Adoring the world of the Lord's glad adorning,
And sing to the glory of Ninety-not-Out.

8

OLD SCOUT

Is it because I'm bent and grey,
    Though wearing rather well,
That I can slickly get away
    With all the yarns I tell?
Is it because my bleary eye
    No longer beams with youth
That I can plant a whopping lie,
    And flout the truth?

I wonder why folks hark to me
    Where once they would have laughed?
They treat my yarns respectfully,
    No matter how they're daft.
They count the notches on my gun
    And stroke its polished butt,
Wanting to know why every one
    Of them was cut.

Indeed were I to stick to fact
    Their interest would flag;
Dramatically I must act
    The rôle of scalliwag;
A battle veteran to be,
    A frozen argonaut,
A castaway in coral sea,—
    Such tommyrot!

And so with unction I conceive
    Invention wild and new,
Until I'm coming to believe
    My taradiddles true . . .
Is it because I'm old and sage,
    I draw a bow that's risky?
Or can it be—that lies with age
    Improve like whisky?

ROVER'S REST

By parents I would not be pinned,
    Nor in my home abide,
For I was wanton as the wind
    And tameless as the tide;
So scornful of domestic hearth,
    And bordered garden path,
I sought the wilder ways of earth,
    The roads of wrath.

It scares me now to think of how
    Foolhardily I fared;
Though mighty scarred of pelt and pow
    A dozen deaths I've dared;
Yet there are trails I would explore,
    And wilds that for me wait . . .
Alas! I'll wander nevermore,—
    The hour's too late.

The folks are at a picture show,
    I smoke my pipe and sigh.
Soft-slippered by the ember's glow
    A baby-sitter I.
Behold! In dressing-gown of *mauve*,
    To comfort reconciled,
A rover rocks the cradle of
    His new grand-child.

LUCINDY JANE

When I was young I was too proud
   To wheel my daughter in her pram.
"It's *infra dig*," I said aloud,—
   But now I'm old, behold I am
Perambulating up and down
   Grand-daughter through the town.

And when I come into the Square,
   Beside the fountain I will stop;
And as to rest I linger there,
   The dames will say: "How do, Grand-pop!
Lucindy Jane with eyes so blue
   Looks more and more like you."

And sure it's pleased as Punch I get,
   And take Lucindy on my knee;
Aye, at the risk of getting wet,
   I blether to the girls a wee:
Then as we have a bottle date
   Home we perambulate.

Gosh! That's the joy of all my day;
   And as I play the part of nurse:
"She's got your nose," I hear them say.
   Thinks I: "Well now, she might have worse."
And how I dream I'll live to see
   A *great-grandchild* upon my knee,
   Whom folks say looks like me!

THE MOTHER

Your children grow from you apart,
    Afar and still afar;
And yet it should rejoice your heart
    To see how glad they are;
In school and sport, in work and play,
    And last, in wedded bliss
How others claim with joy to-day
    The lips you used to kiss.

Your children distant will become,
    And wide the gulf will grow;
The lips of loving will be dumb,
    The trust you used to know
Will in another's heart repose,
    Another's voice will cheer . . .
And you will fondle baby clothes
    And brush away a tear.

But though you are estranged almost,
    And often lost to view,
How you will see a little ghost
    Who ran to cling to you!
Yet maybe children's children will
    Caress you with a smile . . .
Grandmother love will bless you still,—
    Well, just a little while.

BABY SITTER

From torrid heat to frigid cold
   I've rovered land and sea;
And now, with halting heart I hold
   My grandchild on my knee:
Yet while I've eighty years all told,
   Of moons she has but three.

She sleeps, that fragile miniature
   Of future maidenhood;
She will be wonderful, I'm sure,
   As over her I brood;
She is so innocent, so pure,
   I know she will be good.

My way I've won from woe to weal,
   And hard has been the fight;
Yet in my ingle-nook I feel
   A wondrous peace to-night;
And over me serenely steal
   Warm waves of love and light.

"What sloppy stuff!" I hear you say.
   "Give us a lusty song."
Alas! I'm bent and gnarled and grey,—
   My life may not be long:
Yet let its crown of glory be
   This child upon my knee.

ANNUITANT

Oh I am neither rich nor poor,
  No worker I dispoil;
Yet I am glad to be secure
  From servitude and toil.
For with my lifelong savings I
  Have bought annuity;
And so unto the day I die
  I'll have my toast and tea.

When on the hob the kettle sings
  I'll make an amber brew,
And crunch my toast and think of things
  I do not have to do.
In dressing-gown and deep arm-chair
  I'll give the fire a poke;
Then worlds away from cark and care
  I'll smoke and smoke and smoke.

For I believe the very best
  Of Being is the last;
And I will crown with silver zest
  My patience in the past.
Since compensation is the law
  Of life it's up to me
To round the century and draw
  My Life Annuity.

INFIRMITIES

Because my teeth are feebly few
I cannot bolt my grub like you,
But have to chew and chew and chew
    As you can see;
Yet every mouthful seems so good
I would not haste it if I could,
And so I salivate my food
    With ecstasy.

Because my purse is poor in pence
I spend my dough with common-sense,
And live without the least pretence
    In simple state;
The things I can't afford to buy
Might speed the day I have to die,
So pleased with poverty am I
    And bless my fate.

Because my heart is growing tired,
No more by foolish passion fired,
Nor by ambitious hope inspired,
    As in my youth,
I am content to sit and rest,
And prove the last of life's the best,
And ponder with a cheerful zest
    Some saintly truth.

Because I cannot do the things
I used to, comfort round me clings,
And from the moil of market brings
        Me rich release;
So welcome age with tranquil mind;
Even infirmities are kind,
And in our frailing we may find
        Life's crown of peace.

WORK

When twenty-one I loved to dream,
　　And was to loafing well inclined;
Somehow I couldn't get up steam
　　To welcome work of any kind.
While students burned the midnight lamp,
　　With dour ambition as their goad,
I longed to be a gayful tramp
　　And greet adventure on the road.

But now that sixty years have sped,
　　Behold! I toil from morn to night.
The thoughts that teem into my head
　　I pray: God give me time to write.
With eager and unflagging pen
　　No drudgery of desk I shirk,
And preach to all retiring men
　　The gospel of unceasing work.

And yet I do not sadly grieve
　　Such squandering of golden days;
For from my dreaming I believe
　　Have stemmed my least unworthy lays.
Aye, toil is best when all is said,
　　As age has made me understand . . .
So fitly fold, when I am dead,
　　　　　　A pencil in my hand.

A CHARACTER

How often do I wish I were
What people call a *character*;
A ripe and cherubic old chappie
Who lives to make his fellows happy;
With in his eyes a merry twinkle,
And round his lips a laughing wrinkle;
Who radiating hope and cheer
Grows kindlier with every year.

For this ideal let me strive,
And keep the lad in me alive;
Nor argument nor anger know,
But my own way serenely go;
The woes of men to understand,
Yet walk with humour hand in hand;
To love each day and wonder why
Folks are not so jocund as I.

So be you simple, decent, kind,
With gentle heart and quiet mind;
And if to righteous anger stung,
Restrain your temper and your tongue.
Let thought for others be your guide,
And patience triumph over pride . . .
With charity for those who err,
Live life so folks may say you were—
God bless your heart!—*A Character.*

SECOND CHILDHOOD

Some deem I'm gentle, some I'm kind:
It may be so,—I cannot say.
I know I have a simple mind
And see things in a simple way;
And like a child I love to play.

I love to toy with pretty words
And syllable them into rhyme;
To make them sing like sunny birds
In happy droves with silver chime,
In dulcet groves in summer time.

I pray, with hair more white than grey,
And second childhood coming on,
That yet with wonderment I may
See life as in its lucent dawn,
And be by beauty so beguiled
       I'll sing as sings a child.

RHYMES FOR RIBALDRY

THE GHOSTS

Said Lenin's ghost to Stalin's ghost:
    "Mate with me in the Tomb;
Then day by day the rancid host
    May gaze upon our doom.
A crystal casket we will share;
    Come, crusty Comrade come,
And we will bear the public stare,
    Ad nauseum."

Said Stalin's spook to Lenin's spook:
    "Long have you held your place.
The masses must be bored to look
    Upon your chemic face.
A change might be a good idear,
    And though I pity you,
There is within the Tomb, I fear,
    No room for two."

Said Lenin's wraith to Stalin's wraith:
    "You're welcome to my job;
Let millions of our mighty faith
    Gaze on your noble nob.
So when to goodly earth I've gone,
    (And I'll be glad to go),
Your carrion can carry on
    Our waxwork show."

WINE BIBBER

I would rather drink than eat,
　　And though I superbly sup,
Food, I feel, can never beat
　　Delectation of the cup.
Wine it is that crowns the feast;
　　Fish and fowl and fancy meat
Are of my delight the least:
　　I would rather drink than eat.

Though no Puritan I be,
　　And have doubts of Kingdom Come,
With those fellows I agree
　　Who deplore the Demon Rum.
Gin and brandy I decline,
　　And I shy at whisky neat;
But give me rare vintage wine,—
　　Gad! I'd rather drink than eat.

Food surfeit is of the beast;
　　Wine is from the gods a gift.
All from prostitute to priest
　　Can attest to its uplift.
Green and garnet glows the vine;
　　Grapes grow plump in happy heat;
Gold and ruby winks the wine . . .
　　Come! Let's rather drink than eat.

COWARDICE

Although you deem it far from nice,
    And it perchance may hurt you,
Let me suggest that cowardice
    Can masquerade as virtue;
And many a maid remains a maid
    Because she is afraid.

And many a man is chaste because
    He fears the house of sin;
And though before the door he pause,
    He dare not enter in:
So worse than being dissolute
    At home he plays the flute.

And many an old cove such as I
    Is troubled with the jitters,
And being as he's scared to die
    Gives up his gin and bitters;
While dreading stomach ulcers he
    Chucks dinner for high tea.

Well, we are wise. When life begins
    To look so dour and dark
'Tis good to jettison our sins
    And keep afloat the bark:
But don't let us claim lack of vice
    For what's plumb cowardice!

MY CUCKOO CLOCK

I bought a cuckoo clock
        And glad was I
To hear its tick and tock,
        Its dulcet cry.
But Jones, whose wife is young
        And pretty too,
Winced when that bird gave tongue:
        Cuckoo! Cuckoo!

I have a lady friend
        Whom I would wed,
For dalliance should end
        In bridal bed.
Until the thought occurred:
        Can she be true?
And then I heard that bird:
        Cuckoo! Cuckoo!

Though ignorance is bliss
        And love be blind,
Faithless may be the kiss
        Of womankind.
So now sweet echoes mock
        My wish to woo:
Confound that cursed clock!
        Cuckoo! Cuckoo!

PATCHES

Mother focused with a frown
The part of me where I sit down.
Said she: "Your pants are wearing through;
Let me sew on a patch for you."
And so she did,—of azure blue.

My britches were of sober grey,
And when I went to school next day,
The fellows said: "Excuse our smile:
We saw your patch 'way off a mile."
Said I: "Sure, it's the latest style."

So each boy asked his Ma to match
With bluer blue my super-patch,
And when to school they came *en masse,*
It was the emblem of our class,
Admired by every bonnie lass.

Now when I'm old and in my dotage,
I hope I'll have a humble cottage,
And sit me by a hive of bees,
A *patchwork* quilt across my knees,
Warming my worn hands in the sun,
All ropey with the work they've done.

The work they've done to give me this
Brief bit of comfort, ease and bliss;
My pathway edged with cockle shells,
And bright with Canterbury bells,
That leads to where my humble thatch is,
It, too, adorned with straw-bright patches.

TITINE

Although I have a car of class,
    A limousine,
I also have a jenny ass
    I call Titine.
And if I had in sober sense
    To choose between,
I know I'd give the preference
    To sleek Titine.

My chauffeur drives my Cadillac
    In uniform.
I wear a worn coat on my back
    That he would scorn.
He speeds with umpty equine power,
    Like an express;
I amble at eight miles an hour,
    Or even less.

My wife can use our fancy bus
    To cut a dash;
She very definitely does,
    And blows my cash.
But this old codger seeks the sane
    And simple scene;
Content to jog along a lane
    With old Titine.

So as in country ways I go
    Wife loves the town;
But though I'm slow, serene I know
    I won't break down.
With brawn and bone I reckon mine
    The best machine:
Old folks and donkeys best combine,
    —"Giddup, Titine!"

THE SUM-UP

It is not power and fame
        That make success;
It is not rank or name
        Rate happiness.
It is not honour due
        Nor pile of pelf:
The pay-off is: Did you
        Enjoy yourself?

A pal of days gone by
        I reckon more
Of a success than I
        Who've gold in store.
His life, though none too long,
        Was never dull:
Of woman, wine and song
        Bill had his full.

Friend, you are a success
        If you can say:
"A heap of happiness
        Has come my way.
No cheers have made me glad,
        No wealth I've won;
But oh how I have had
        A heap of FUN!"

THE MACARONIS

Italian people peaceful are,—
   Let it be to their credit.
They mostly fail to win a war,
   —Oh they themselves have said it.
"Allergic we to lethal guns
   And military might:
We love our homes and little ones,
     And loathe to fight."

But Teutons are a warrior race
   Who seek the sword to rattle;
And in the sun they claim a place,
   Even at price of battle.
The prestige of a uniform
   Is sacred in their sight;
They deem that they are soldiers born
     And might is right.

And so I love Italians though
   Their fighting powers are petty;
My heart with sympathy doth go
   To eaters of spaghetti.
And if the choice were left to me,
   I know beyond a doubt
A hundred times I'd rather be
     A Dago than a Kraut.

MY FAVOURED FARE

Some poets sing of scenery;
Some to fair maids make sonnets sweet.
A fig for love and greenery,
Be mine a song of things to eat.
Let brother bards divinely dream,
I'm just plain human, as you see;
And choose to carol such a theme
             As ham and eggs and tea.

Just two fried eggs or maybe three,
With lacy rims and sunside up,
Pink coral ham and amber tea
Poured in a big, fat china cup.
I have no crave for finer fare;
That's just the chuck for chaps like me.
Aye, if I were a millionaire—
             Just ham and eggs and tea.

When of life's fussiness I tire,
And on my skull I wear a cap,
As tartan-shawled beside the fire
I stroke the kitten on my lap:
Give me no broth and chicken breast;
My last repast shall hearty be . . .
Oh how I'll sup with chuckling zest
             On ham and eggs and tea!

IMMORTALITY

Full well I trow that when I die
    Down drops the curtain;
Another show is all my eye
    And Betty Martin.
I know the score, and with a smile
    Of rueful rating,
I reckon I am not worth while
    Perpetuating.

I hope that God,—if God there be
    Of love and glory,
Will let me off Eternity,
    And end my story.
Will count me just a worn-out bit
    Of human matter,
Who's done his job or bungled it,
    —More like the latter.

I did not beg for mortal breath,
    Plus hell or Heaven;
So let the last pay-off be death,
    And call it even.
To Nature I will pay my debt
    With stoic laughter:
But spare me, God, your awful threat
    Of Life Here-after!

INTOLERANCE

I have no brief for gambling, nay
    The notion I express
That money earned 's the only way
    To pay for happiness.
With cards and dice I do not hold;
    By betting I've been bit:
Conclusion: to get honest gold
    You've got to sweat for it.

Though there be evil in strong drink
    It's brought me heaps of fun;
And now, with some reserve, I think
    My toping days are done.
Though at teetotal cranks I laugh,
    Yet being sound and hale,
I find the best of drinks to quaff
    Is good old Adam's ale.

I do not like your moralist,
    Who with a righteous grin
Informs you o'er a pounding fist:
    "Unchastity is sin."
I don't believe it, but I grant,
    By every human test,
From parson, pimp and maiden aunt,
    Morality is best.

Yet what a bore our lives would be
    If we lived as we should;
It's such a blessing to be free,
    And not be over-good.
I value virtues great and small,
    As I in life advance:
But O the greatest sin of all
    I count—INTOLERANCE.

PERFECTION

If I could practise what I preach,
Of fellows there would few be finer;
If I were true to what I teach
My life would be a lot diviner.
If I would act the way I speak,
Of halo I might be a winner:
The spirit wills, the flesh is weak,—
     I'm just a simple sinner.

Six days I stray,—on number seven
I try to be a little better,
And stake a tiny claim on Heaven
By clinging close to gospel letter.
My pew I occupy on Sunday,
And though I draw the line at snoring,
I must admit I long for Monday,
     And find the sermon boring.

Although from godly grace I fall,
For sensed with sin my every act is,
'Twere better not to preach at all,
Then I would have no need to practice.
So Sabbath day I'll sneak away,
And though the Church grieve my defection,
In sunny woodland I will pray:
     "God save us from Perfection!"

THE APE AND I

Said a monkey unto me:
"How I'm glad I am not you!
See, I swing from tree to tree,
Something that you cannot do.
In gay greenery I drown;
Swift to skyey heights I scale:
As you watch me hang head down
Don't you wish you had a tail?

"Don't you wish that you could wear
In the place of stuffy clothes,
Just a silky coat of hair,
Never shoes to cramp your toes?
Never need to toil for bread,
Round you nuts and fruit and spice;
And with palm tuft for a bed
Happily to crack your lice?"

Said I: "You are right, maybe;
Witting naught of worldly woe,
Gloriously you are free,
And of death you nothing know.
Envying your monkey mind,
Innocent of blight and bale,
As I touch my bald behind
How I wish I had a tail!"

So in toils of trouble caught,
Oft I wonder with a sigh
If that blue-bummed ape is not
Happier than I?

DEATH OF A COCKROACH

I opened wide the bath-room door,
And all at once switched on the light,
When moving swift across the floor
I saw a streak of ebon bright:
Then quick, with slipper in my hand,
Before it could escape,—I slammed.

I missed it once, I missed it twice,
But got it ere it gained its lair.
I fear my words were far from nice,
Though d——s with me are rather rare:
Then lo! I thought that dying roach
Regarded me with some reproach.

Said I: "Don't think I grudge you breath;
I hate to spill your greenish gore,
But why did you invite your death
By straying on my bath-room floor?"
"It is because," said he (or she),
"Adventure is my destiny.

"By evolution I was planned,
As marvellously made as you;
And I am led to understand
The selfsame God conceived us two:
Sire, though the *coup de grâce* you give,
Even a roach has right to live."

Said I: "Of course you have a right,—
But not to blot my bath-room floor.
Yet though with slipper I may smite,
Your doom I morally deplore . . .
From cellar gloom to stellar space
Let bards and beetles have their place.

A SONG FOR KILTS

How grand the human race would be
  If every man would wear a kilt,
A flirt of Tartan finery,
  Instead of trousers, custom built!
Nay, do not think I speak to joke:
  (You know I'm not that kind of man),
I am convinced that all men folk.
  Should wear the costume of a Clan.

Imagine how it's braw and clean
  As in the wind it flutters free;
And so conducive to hygiene
  In its sublime simplicity.
No fool fly-buttons to adjust,—
  Wi' shanks and maybe buttocks bare;
Oh chiels, just take my word on trust,
  A bonny kilt's the only wear.

'Twill save a lot of siller too,
  (And here a canny Scotsman speaks),
For one good kilt will wear you through
  A half-a-dozen pairs of breeks.
And how it's healthy in the breeze!
  And how it swings with saucy tilt!
How lassies love athletic knees
  Below the waggle of a kilt!

True, I just wear one in my mind,
  Since sent to school by Celtic aunts,
When girls would flip it up behind,
  Until I begged for lowland pants.
But now none dare do that to me,
  And so I sing with lyric lilt,—
How happier the world would be
  If every male would wear a kilt!

VIOLET DE VERE

You've heard of Violet de Vere, strip-teaser of renown,
Whose sitting-base out-faired the face of any girl in
town;
Well, she was haled before the Bench for breachin' of
the Peace,
Which signifies araisin' Cain, an' beatin' up the police.
So there she stood before the Court of ruddy Judge Mc-
Graw,
Whom folks called Old Necessity, because he knew no
law.
Aye, crackin' in a silken gown, an' sheddin' of a tear,
Ashine wi' gold an' precious stones sat Violet de Vere.

Old Judge McGraw looked dourly down an' stroked his
silver beard.
Says he: "Although the Sheriff's bruised, the lady
should be heared.
What can you say in your defence? We'll give you a
square deal."
"I jest forget," said Violet. "Maybe it was my heel.
I always want to kick the gong when I am feelin' gay;
It's most unfortunate, I guess, his face was in the way."
Then scratchin' of his snowy pow the Judge looked
down severe,
Where bright wi' paint like plaster saint sat Violet de
Vere.

Says he: "I'm going to impose a twenty dollar fine."

Says Violet: "Your Honour, to your judgement I re-
sign.

I realize I should not my agility reveal:

Next time I'll kick the Sheriff with my toe and not my
heel.

I'm grateful to the Court because I'm not put in the
clink;

There's twenty plunks to pay my fine,—but now I
come to think:

Judge, darlin', you've been owin' me five bucks for near
a year:

Take fifteen,—there! We'll call it square," said Violet
de Vere.

RHYMES FOR REALITY

VISIBILITY

Because my eyes were none too bright
  Strong spectacles I bought,
And lo! there sprang into my sight
  A life beyond my thought:
A world of wonder and delight
  My magic lenses brought.

Aye, sudden leaping in my sight
  The far became the near;
Life unbelievably was bright,
  And vividly was clear.
My heart was lifted with delight,
  Then—then I shrank in fear.
For faces I had thought were gay
  I saw were lined with care,
While strange corruption and decay
  Surprised me everywhere:
Dismayed I put my specs away,—
  Such truth I could not bear.

And now I do not want to see
  With clarity of view;
For while there's heaven hell may be
  More tragically true:
Though dim may be Reality,
  Sheer love shines through.

THE TWINS OF LUCKY STRIKE

I've sung of Violet de Vere, that slinky, minky dame,
Of Gertie of the Diamond Tooth, and Touch-the-Button Nell,
And Maye Lamore,—at eighty-four I oughta blush wi' shame
That in my wild and wooly youth I knew them ladies well.
And Klondike Kit, and Gumboot Sue, and many I've forgot;
They had their faults, as I recall, the same as you and me;
But come to take them all in all, the daisy of the lot,
The glamour queen of dance-hall dames was Montreal Maree.

And yet her heart was bigger than a barn, the boys would say;
Always the first to help the weak, and so with words of woe,
She put me wise that Lipstick Lou was in the family way:
"An' who ze baby's fazzaire ees, only ze bon Dieu know."
Then on a black and bitter night passed on poor Lipstick Lou;
And by her bedside, midwife wise, wi' tears aflowin' free,
A holdin' out the newly born,—an' by gosh! there was *two*:
"Helas! I am zere mossaire now," said Montreal Maree.

Said One-eyed Mike: "In Lucky Strike we've never
  yet had twins,"
As darin' inundation he held one upon each knee.
"Say, boys, ain't they a purty sight, as like's a pair o'
  pins—
We gotta hold a christinin' wi' Father Tim McGee."
"I aim to be their Godpa," bellowed Black Moran from
  Nome.
The guy wot don't love childer is a blasted S.O.B.:
So long as I can tot a gun them kids won't lack a
  home."
"I sink zey creep into my heart," said Montreal Maree.

'Twas hectic in the Nugget Bar, the hooch was flowin'
  free,
An Lousetown Liz was singin' of how someone done
  her wrong,
Wi' sixty seeded sourdoughs all ahollerin' their glee,
When One-eyed Mike uprose an' called suspension of
  the song.
Says he: "Aloodin' to them twins, their age in months
  is two,
An' I propose wi' Christmas close, we offer them a tree.
'Twill sure be mighty pleasin' to the ghost o' Lipstick
  Lou . . ."
"Zen you will be ze Père Noël," said Montreal Maree.

The dance hall of the Nugget Bar erupted joy an' light,
An' set upon the stage them twins was elegant to see,
Like angel cherubs in their robes of pure baptismal
    white,
Abaskin' in the sunny smile o' Father Tim McGee.
Then on the bar stood Santa Claus, says he: "We'll
    form a Trust;
So all you sourdoughs heft your pokes an' hang 'em
    on the Tree.
To give them kids a chance in life we'll raise enough
    or bust!"
"For zem I pray ze Lord to bless," said Montreal
    Maree.

You never saw a Christmas Tree so swell as that, I vow,
Wi' sixty sweaty sourdoughs ringin' round them in-
    fants two;
Their solid pokes o' virgin gold aweighin' down each
    bough,
All singin' *Christ Is Risen,* for the soul o' Lipstick Lou,
"Lo! Death is a deliverer, the purger of our sins,
And Motherhood leads up to God," said Father Tim
    McGee.
Then all the Ladies of the Line bent down to kiss them
    twins,
Clasped to the breast, Madonna-like, of Montreal
    Maree.

Sure 'tis the love of childer makes for savin' of the soul,
And in Maternity the hope of humankind we see;
So though she wears no halo, headin' out for Heaven's
goal,
Awheelin' of a double pram,—bless Montreal Maree!

CHILD LOVER

Drunk or sober Uncle Jim
  Played the boy;
Never glum or sour or grim,
  Oozin' joy.
Most folks thought he was no good,
  Blamin' him;
But where kiddies were, you could
  Bank on Jim.

Sure he allus hated work,
  Lovin' play.
"Jest a good fer nuthin' jerk,"
  Lots would say.
Yet how children fell for him,
  Whooped with glee:
Guys so popular as Jim
  Seldom be.

How old songs, sweet as a bell,
  He would sing!
What grand stories he would tell,
  Gesturin'!
Elders reckoned him a sot,
  Sighin' sad;
But with tiny toddlers what
  Sport he had!

Might have had a brood, they said,
    Of his own;
Lost his wife in childbirth bed,
    Left him lone . . .
Well, now he is cold an' still,
    Here's to him:
Kids an' mothers always will
    Bless old Jim.

GRAND-PA'S WHIM

While for me gapes the greedy grave
        It don't make sense
That I should have a crazy crave
        To paint our fence.
Yet that is what I aim to do,
        Though dim my sight:
Jest paint them aged pickets blue,
        Or green or white.

Jest squat serenely in the sun
        Wi' brush an' paint,
An' gay them pickets one by one,
        —A chore! It ain't.
The job is joy. Although I'm slow
        I save expense:
So folks, let me before I go,
        Smart that ol' fence.

Them pickets with my hands I made,
        When young and spry;
I coloured them a gleeful shade
        To glad the eye.
So now as chirpy as a boy,
        'Ere I go hence,
Once more let me jest bright to joy
        Our picket fence.

BIRDS OF A FEATHER

Of bosom friends I've had but seven,
    Despite my years are ripe;
I hope they're now enjoying Heaven,
    Although they're not the type;
Nor, candidly, no more am I,
    Though overdue to die.

For looking back I see that they
    Were weak and wasteful men;
They loved a sultry jest alway,
    And women now and then.
They smoked and gambled, soused and swore,
    —Yet no one was a bore.

'Tis strange I took to lads like these,
    On whom the good should frown;
Yet all with poetry would please
    To wash his wassail down;
Their temples touched the starry way,
    But O what feet of clay!

Well, all are dust, of fame bereft;
    They bore a cruel cross,
And I, the canny one, am left,—
    Yet as I grieve their loss,
I deem, because they loved me well,
    They'll welcome me in Hell.

OLD CRONY

I had a friend, a breezy friend
    I liked an awful lot;
And in his company no end
    Of happiness I got.
We clicked in temper, taste and mood,
    We gypsied side by side,—
And then, as no pal ever should,
        He upped and died.

A score of years have since gone by,
    Yet I bemoan him still;
He used to call me Bob and I
    Was wont to call him Bill.
Oh how I wish that he were here,
    How we would bravely walk
On heather hills to tavern cheer,
        And talk and talk!

If as he always used to do,
    He'd just drop in to tea,
To rest awhile and jest awhile,
    How chirpy I would be!
Then he would puff his pipe of briar
    And I my cigarette,
And we would yarn beside the fire,
        And time forget.

Old Pal, come back a little while,
    If just to let me say
How much I miss your jolly smile
    Now you have gone away.
Ah, when in life's allotted span
    We near our journey's end,
What greater treasure is there than
    A Golden Friend!

OLD BOB

I guess folks think I'm mighty dumb
      Since Jack and Jim and Joe
Have hit the trail to Kingdom Come
      And left me here below:
Since Death, the bastard, bowled them out,
      And left me faced with—Doubt.

My pals have all passed out on me
      And I am by my lone;
Old Bill was last, and now I see
      His name cut on a stone;
A marble slab, but not as fine
      As I have picked for mine.

I nurse and curse rheumatic pain
      As on the porch I sit;
With nothing special in my brain
      I rock and smoke and spit:
When one is nearing to the end
      One sorely needs a friend.

My Pals have gone,—in God's good earth
      I guess they're packed up snug,
And since I have no guts for mirth
      I zipper up my mug:
The question that I ponder on
      Is—where the heck they've gone?

PLAYBOY

I greet the challenge of the dawn
    With weary, bleary eyes;
Into the sky so ashen wan
    I wait the sun to rise;
Then in the morning's holy hush,
    With heart of shame I hear
A robin from a lilac bush
    Pipe pure and clear.

All night in dive and dicing den,
    With wantons and with wine
I've squandered on wild, witless men
    The fortune that was mine;
The gold my father fought to save
    In folly I have spent;
And now to fill a pauper's grave
    My steps are bent.

See! how the sky is amber bright!
    The thrushes thrill their glee.
The dew-drops sparkle with delight,
    And yonder smiles the sea.
Oh let me plunge to drown the pain
    Of love and faith forgot:
Then purged I may return again,
    —Or I may not.

CLASS-MATES

Bob Briggs went in for Government,
    And helps to run the State;
Some day they say he'll represent
    His party in debate:
But with punk politics his job,
    I do not envy Bob.

Jim Jones went in for writing books,
    Best sellers were his aim;
He's ten years younger than he looks,
    And licks the heels of Fame:
Though shop-girls make a fuss of him
    I do not envy Jim.

Joe Giles went in for grabbing gold,
    And grovelled in the dirt;
He, too, looks prematurely old,
    His gastric ulcers hurt:
Although he has a heap of dough.
    I do not envy Joe.

I've neither fame nor power nor wealth,
    I fish and hunt for food;
But I have heaps of rugged health,
    And life seems mighty good.
So when my class-mates come to spend
    A week-end in my shack,
With lake and wood at journey's end
    —They envy Jack.

THE DAMNED

My days are haunted by the thought
Of men in coils of Justice caught
With stone and steel, in chain and cell,
Of men condemned to living hell,—
      Yet blame them not.

In my sun-joy their dark I see:
For what they are and *had* to be
Blame Nature, red in tooth and claw,
Blame laws beyond all human law,
      —Blame Destiny.

Behind blind walls I see them go,
Grim spectres of eternal woe,
Drained grey of hope, dead souls of self-slain,—
And yet I know with pang of pain
      It must be so.

I know that brother's blood they've spilt,
And sons of Cain must pay their guilt;
I know the deviltries that stem
From dark abyss we *must* condemn;
I know that but for heaven's grace
We might be rotting in their place:
      —God pity them!

MY BROTHERS

While I make rhymes my brother John
Makes shiny shoes which dames try on,
And finding to their fit and stance
They buy and wear with elegance;
But mine is quite another tale,—
    For song there is no sale.

My brother Tom a tailor shop
Is owner of, and ladies stop
To try the models he has planned,
And richly pay, I understand:
Yet not even a dingy dime
Can I make with my rhyme.

My brother Jim sells stuff to eat
Like trotters, tripe and sausage meat.
I dare not by his window stop,
Lest he should offer me a chop;
For though a starving bard I be,
To hell, say I, with charity!

My brothers all are proud of purse,
But though my poverty I curse,
I would not for a diadem
Exchange my lowly lot with them:
A garret and a crust for me,
And reams and dreams of Poetry.

BILL'S PRAYER

I never thought that Bill could say
　　　　A proper prayer;
'Twas more in his hard-bitten way
　　　　To cuss and swear;
Yet came the night when Baby Ted
　　　　Was bitter ill,
I tip-toed to his tiny bed,
　　　　And there was Bill.

Aye, down upon his bended knees
　　　　I heard him cry:
"O God, don't take my kiddy, please!
　　　　Don't let him die!"
Then softly so he would not see,
　　　　I shrank away:
He would have been so shamed for me
　　　　To see him pray.

Men-folk are queer: Bill acts up tough,
　　　　Yet how it's odd,
When things are looking downright rough
　　　　He tunes to God.
"The Parson and the Priest be darned!"
　　　　I've heard him say:
Yet when his baby is concerned
　　　　He's quick to pray.

Maybe it's gentle parent-hood
　　　That gives us grace,
And in its sacrificial mood
　　　Uplifts the race.
Of sentiment, all self above,
　　　That goodness sums
I think the saving best is Love
　　　For little ones.

THE SILENT ONES

I'm just an ordinary chap
    Who comes home to his tea,
And mostly I don't care a rap
    What people think of me;
I do my job and take my pay,
    And love of peace expound;
But as I go my patient way,
      —Don't push me round.

Though I respect authority
    And order never flout,
When Law and Justice disagree
    You can include me out.
The Welfare State I tolerate
    If it is kept in bound,
But if you wish to rouse my hate
      —Just push me round.

And that's the way with lots of us:
    We want to *feel* we're free;
So labour governments we cuss
    And mock at monarchy.
Yea, we are men of secret mirth,
    And fury seldom sound;
But if you value peace on earth
      —Don't push us round.

ADOPTION

Because I was a woman lone
    And had of friends so few,
I made two little ones my own,
    Whose parents no one knew;
Unwanted foundlings of the night,
    Left at the Convent door,
Whose tiny hands in piteous plight
        Seemed to implore.

By Deed to them I gave my name,
    And never will they know
That from the evil slums they came,
    Two waifs of want and woe;
I fostered them with love and care
    As if they were my own:
Now John, my son, is tall and fair,
        And dark is Joan.

My boy's a member of the Bar,
    My girl a nurse serene;
Yet when I think of what they are
    And what they might have been,
With shuddering I glimpse a hell
    Of black and bitter fruit . . .
Where John might be a criminal,
        And Joan—a prostitute.

MARIE ANTOINETTE

They told to Marie Antoinette:
    "The beggars at your gate
Have eyes too sad for tears to wet,
    And for your pity wait."
But Marie only laughed and said:
    "My heart they will not ache:
If people starve for want of bread
        Let them eat cake."

The Court re-echoed her *bon mot*;
    It rang around the land,
Till masses wakened from their woe
    With scythe and pick in hand.
It took a careless, callous phrase
    To rouse a folk forlorn:
A million roared the Marseillaise:
        Freedom was born.

And so to Marie Antoinette
    Let's pay a tribute due;
Humanity owes her a debt,
    (Ironical, it's true).
She sparked world revolution red,
    And as with glee they bore
Upon a pike her lovely head
        —Her curls dripped gore.

THE VISIONARY

If fortune had not granted me
　　To suck the Muse's teats,
I think I would have liked to be
　　A sweeper of the streets;
And city gutters glad to groom,
　　Have heft a bonny broom.

There—as amid the crass and crush
　　The limousines swished by,
I would have leaned upon my brush
　　With visionary eye:
Deeming despite their loud allure
　　That I was rich, they poor.

Aye, though in garb terrestrial,
　　To Heaven I would pray,
And dream with broom celestial
　　I swept the Milky Way;
And golden chariots would ring,
　　And harps of Heaven sing.

And all the strumpets passing me,
　　And heelers of the Ward
Would glorified Madonnas be,
　　And angels of the Lord;
And all the brats in gutters grim
　　Be rosy cherubim.

THE WIDOW

I don't think men of eighty odd
    Should let a surgeon operate;
Better to pray for peace with God,
    And reconcile oneself to Fate:
At four-score years we really should
    Be quite prepared to go for good.

That's what I told my husband but
    He had a hearty lust for life,
And so he let a surgeon cut
    Into his innards with a knife.
The sawbones swore: "The man's so fat
    His kidneys take some getting at."

And then (according to a nurse),
    They heard him petulantly say:
"Adipose tissue is a curse:
    It's hard to pack them tripes away."
At last he did; sewed up the skin,
    But left, some say, a swab within.

I do not doubt it could be so,
    For Lester did not long survive.
But for mishap, I think with woe
    My hubby might be still alive.
And while they praise the surgeon's skill,
    My home I've sold—to pay his bill.

SLUGGING SAINT

'Twas in a pub in Battersea
    They call the "Rose and Crown,"
Quite suddenly, it seemed to me,
    The Lord was looking down;
The Lord was looking from above,
    And shiny was His face,
And I was filled with gush of love
    For all the human race.

Anon I saw three ancient men
    Who reckoned not of bliss,
And they looked quite astonished when
    I gave each one a kiss.
I kissed each on his balding spot
    With heart of Heaven grace . . .
And then it seemed there was a lot
    Of trouble round the place.

They had me up before the beak,
    But though I told my tale,
He sentenced me to spend a week
    In Yard of Scotland Gaol.
So when they kindly set me free
    Please don't think it amiss,
If Battling Bill of Battersea,
    For love of all humanity
        Gives *you* a kiss.

SEGREGATION

I stood beside the silken rope,
   Five dollars in my hand,
And waited in my patient hope
   To sit anear the Band,
And hear the famous Louie play
   The best hot trumpet of today.

And then a waiter loafing near
   Says in a nasty tone:
"Old coon, we don't want darkies here,
   Beat it before you're thrown."
So knowin' nothin' I could do
   I turned to go and—there was Lou.

I think he slapped that Dago's face;
   His voice was big an' loud;
An' then he leads me from my place
   Through all that tony crowd.
World-famous Louie by the hand
   Took me to meet his famous Band.

"Listen, you folks," I heard him say.
   "Here's Grand-papa what's come.
Savin' he teached me how to play,
   I mighta been a bum.
Come on, Grand-pop, git up an' show
   How you kin trumpet *Ol' Black Joe*."

Tremblin' I played before his Band:
   You should have heard the cheers.
Them swell folks gave me such a hand
   My cheeks was wet wi' tears . . .
An' now I'm off to tell the wife
   The proudest night o' all ma life.

OLD TOM

The harridan who holds the inn
　　At which I toss a pot,
Is old and uglier than sin,—
　　I'm glad she knows me not.
Indeed, for me it's hard to think,
　　Although my pow's like snow,
She was the lass so fresh and pink
　　I courted long ago.

I wronged her, yet it's sadly true
　　She wanted to be wronged:
They mostly do, although 'tis you,
　　The male bloke who is thonged.
Well, anyway I left her then
　　To sail across the sea,
And no doubt she had other men,
　　And soon lost sight of me.

So now she is a paunchy dame
　　And mistress of the inn,
With temper tart and tongue to blame,
　　Moustache and triple chin.
And though I have no proper home
　　Contentedly I purr,
And from my whiskers wipe the foam,
　　—Glad I did not wed her.

Yet it's so funny sitting here
   To stare into her face;
And as I raise my mug of beer
   I dream of our disgrace.
And so I come and come each day
   To more and more enjoy
The joke—that fifty years away
   I was her honey boy.

RHYMES FOR RUSTICITY

LEARN TO LIKE

School yourself to savour most
Joys that have but little cost;
Prove the best of life is free,
Sun and stars and sky and sea;
Eager in your eyes to please,
Proffer meadows, brooks and trees;
Nature strives for your content,
Never charging you a cent.

Learn to love a garden gay,
Flowers and fruit in rich array.
Care for dogs and singing birds,
Have for children cheery words.
Find plain food and comfort are
More than luxury by far.
Music, books and honest friends
Outweigh golden dividends.

Love your work and do it well,
Scorning not a leisure spell.
Hold the truest form of wealth
Body fit and ruddy health.
Let your smile of happiness
Rustic peace serenely stress:
Home to love and heart to pray—
Thank your God for every day.

MY INNER LIFE

'Tis true my garments threadbare are,
            And sorry poor I seem;
But inly I am richer far
            Than any poet's dream.
For I've a hidden life no one
            Can ever hope to see;
A sacred sanctuary none
            May share with me.

Aloof I stand from out the strife,
            Within my heart a song;
By virtue of my inner life
            I to myself belong.
Against man-ruling I rebel,
            Yet do not fear defeat,
For to my secret citadel
            I may retreat.

Oh you who have an inner life
            Beyond this dismal day
With wars and evil rumours rife,
            Go blessedly your way.
Your refuge hold inviolate;
            Unto yourself be true,
And shield serene from sordid fate
            The Real You.

INNOCENCE

The height of wisdom seems to me
        That of a child;
So let my ageing vision be
        Serene and mild.
The depth of folly, I aver,
        Is to fish deep
In that dark pool of science where
        Truth-demons sleep.

Let me not be a bearded sage
        Seeing too clear;
In issues of the atom age
        Man-doom I fear.
So long as living's outward show
        To me is fair,
What lies behind I do not know,
        And do not care.

Of woeful fears of future ill
        That earth-folk haunt,
Let me, as radiant meadow rill,
        Be ignorant.
Aye, though a sorry dunce I be
        In learning's school,
Lord, marvellously make of me
        Your Happy Fool!

TRANQUILLITY

Oh if it were not for my wife
    And family increase,
How gladly would I close my life
    In monastery peace!
A sweet and scented isle I know
    Where monks in muteness dwell,
And there in sereness I would go
    And seek a cell.

On milk and oaten meal I'd live,
    With carrot, kail and cheese;
The greens that tiny gardens give,
    The bounty of the bees.
Then war might rage, I would not know,
    Or knowing would not care:
No echo of a world of woe
    Would irk me there.

And I would be forgotten too
    As mankind I forgot;
Read Shakespeare and the Bible through,
    And brood in quiet thought.
Content with birds and trees and flowers
    In mellow age to find
'Mid monastery's holy hours
    God's Peace of Mind.

AWAKE TO SMILE

When I blink sunshine in my eyes
 And hail the amber morn,
Before the rosy dew-drop dries
 With sparkle on the thorn;
When boughs with robin rapture ring,
 And bees hum in the may,—
Then call me young, with heart of Spring,
  Though I be grey.

But when no more I know the joy
 And urgence of that hour,
As like a happy-hearted boy
 I leap to land aflower;
When gusto I no longer feel,
 To rouse with glad hooray,—
Then call me old and let me steal
  From men away.

Let me awaken with a smile
 And go to garden glee,
For there is such a little while
 Of living left to me;
But when star-wist I frail away,
 Lord, let the hope beguile
That to Ecstatic Light I may
  Awake to smile.

WONDER

For failure I was well equipped
   And should have come to grief,
By atavism grimly gripped,
   A fool beyond belief.
But lo! the Lord was good to me,
   And with a heart to sing,
He gave me to a rare degree
   The Gift of Wondering.

I could not play a stalwart part
   My shoddy soul to save,
And should have gone with broken heart
   A beggar to the grave;
But praise to my anointed sight
   As wandering I went,
I sang of living with delight
   In terms of Wonderment.

Aye, starry-eyed did I rejoice
   With marvel of a child,
And there were those who heard my voice
   Although my words were wild:
So as I go my wistful way,
   With worship let me sing,
And treasure to my farewell day
   God's Gift of Wondering.

SIMPLICITY

What I seek far yet seldom find
Is large simplicity of mind
         In fellow men;
For I have sprouted from the sod,
Like Bobbie Burns, my earthy god,
         —From plough to pen.

So I refuse my brain to vex
With problems prosy and complex,
         Beyond my scope;
To me simplicity is peace,
So I pursue it without cease,
         And growing hope.

"The world is too much with us," wrote
Wise Wordsworth, whom I love to quote,
         When rhymes are coy;
And simple is the world I see,
With bud and bloom and brook and tree
         To give me joy.

So blissfully I slip away
From brazen and dynamic day
         To dingle cool . . .
Now tell me friend, if in your eyes,
By being simple I am wise,—
         Or just a fool?

ELEMENTALIST

Could Fate ordain a lot for me
      Beyond all human ills,
I think that I would choose to be
      A shepherd of the hills;
With shaggy cloak and cape where skies
      Eternally are blue
How I would stare with quiet eyes
      At passing you!

And you would stare at static me,
      Beside my patient flock;
And I would watch you silently,
      A one with time and rock.
Then foreign farings you would chart,
      And fly with fearsome wings,
While I would bide to be a part
      Of elemental things.

Yet strangely I would have it so,
      Since I am kin to these,—
To heather heath and bloom ablow,
      And peaks and piney trees.
As diamond star at evenfall,
      And pearly morning mist
Sing in my veins, myself I call
      An Elementalist.

So as in city dirt and din
        I push a grubby pen,
And toil, my bed and board to win,
        I hate the haunts of men.
Beyond brick wall I seem to see
        Fern dells and rocky rills . . .
O crazy dream! O God, to be
        A shepherd of the hills!

NEIGHBOURS

My neighbour has a field of wheat
        And I a rood of vine;
And he will give me bread to eat,
        And I will give him wine.
And so we are a jolly pair,
        Contentedly unwed,
Singing with supper as we share
        Red wine and crusty bread.

Now venison is mighty meat
        And so is trout and hare;
A mallard duck is sweet to eat
        And quail is dainty fare.
But such are foods for festal day,
        And we will not repine
While on the table we can lay
        Crisp bread and rosy wine.

A will to till one's own of soil
        Is worth a kingly crown,
With bread to feed the belly need,
        And wine to wash it down.
So with my neighbour I rejoice
        That we are fit and free,
Content to praise with lusty voice
        Bread, Wine and Liberty.

MY TRINITY

For all good friends who care to read,
Here let me lyre my living creed . . .

One: you may deem me Pacifist,
For I've no sympathy with strife.
Like hell I hate the iron fist,
And shun the battle-ground of life.
The hope of peace is dear to me,
And I to Christian faith belong,
Holding that breath should sacred be,
      And War is *always* wrong.

Two: Universalist am I
And dream a world that's frontier free,
With common tongue and common tie,
Uncurst by nationality;
Where colour, creed and class are one,
And lowly folk are lifted high;
Where every breed beneath the sun
      Is equal in God's eye.

Three: you may call me Naturist,
For green glade is my quiet quest;
The path of progress I have missed,
And shun the city's sore unrest.
A world that's super-civilized
Is one of worry, want and woe;
In leafy lore let me be wised
      And back to Nature go.

Well, though you may but half agree,
Behold my trusty Trinity.

THE LEARNER

I've learned—Of all the friends I've won
        Dame Nature is the best,
And to her like a child I run
        Craving her mother breast
To comfort me in soul distress,
        And in green glade to find
Far from the world's unloveliness
        Pure peace of mind.

I've learned—the worth of simple ways,
        And though I've loved to roam,
I know the glow of hearth ablaze,
        The bliss of coming home.
I'd rather wear old clothes than new,
        I'd rather walk than drive,
And as my wants are oh so few
        I joy to be alive.

I've learned—that happiness is all,
        A sweetness of the mind;
And would you purge your heart of gall,—
        Try being kind.
Then when some weaker one you aid,
        Believe it true
'Tis God Himself will make the grade
        Less hard for you.

HOUSES

The ivied house was shy and strange
Because I was not used to it;
It seemed as if it hated change
Of ownership, yet bit by bit
        It moulded to my fit.

And then with kindly gravity
And tenderness it tucked me in,
Just like a mother, shielding me
From cold and damp and dust and din,
        Seeking my heart to win.

And now the ivied house and I
Are gently welded into one;
Yet when in cyprus shade I lie,
With smiling it will greet the sun,
        Although my race be run.

For flesh will rot but stone will stay,
And though its walls I hold in fee,
They will be sunnyful and gay
Long after I have ceased to be,
        Forgetting me.

Houses give love to those who love
And care for them and call them Home;
A rosy roof is blest above
The glory of a golden dome:
Let humble hearth-fire close our days
    In peace and praise!

IGNORANCE

Oh happy he who cannot see
   With scientific eyes;
Who does not know how flowers grow,
   And is not planet wise;
Content to find with simple mind
   Joys as they are:
To whom a rose is just a rose,
        A star—a star.

It is not good, I deem, to brood
   On things beyond our ken;
A rustic I would live and die,
   Aloof from learned men;
And laugh and sing with zest of Spring
   In life's exultant scene,—
For vain may be philosophy,
   And what does *meaning* mean?

I'm talking rot,—I'm really not
   As dumb as I pretend;
But happiness, I dimly guess,
   Is what counts in the end.
To educate is to dilate
   The nerves of pain:
So let us give up books and live
   Like hinds again.

The best of wisdom surely is
    To be not overwise;
For may not thought be evil fraught,
    And truth less kind than lies?
So let me praise the golden days
    I played a gay guitar,
And deemed a rose was just a rose,
        A star—a star.

THE WOMB

Up from the evil day
Of wattle and of woad,
Along man's weary way
Dark Pain has been the goad.
Back from the age of stone,
Within his brutish brain,
What pleasure he has known
         Is ease from Pain.

Behold in Pain the force
That haled Man from the Pit,
And set him such a course
No mind can measure it.
To angel from the ape
No human pang was vain
In that divine escape
         To joy through Pain.

See Pain with stoic eyes
And patient fortitude,
A blessing in disguise,
An instrument of good.
Aye, though with hearts forlorn
We to despair be fain,
Believe that Joy is born
         From Womb of Pain.

MUD

Mud is Beauty in the making,
Mud is melody awaking;
Laughter, leafy whisperings,
Butterflies with rainbow wings;
Baby babble, lover's sighs,
Bobolink in lucent skies;
Ardours of heroic blood
All stem back to Matrix Mud.

Mud is mankind in the moulding,
Heaven's mystery unfolding;
Miracles of mighty men,
Raphael's brush and Shakespeare's pen;
Sculpture, music, all we owe
Mozart, Michael Angelo;
Wonder, worship, dreaming spire,
Issue out of primal mire.

In the raw, red womb of Time
Man evolved from cosmic slime;
And our thaumaturgic day
Had its source in ooze and clay . . .
But I have not power to see
Such stupendous alchemy:
And in star-bright lily bud
Lo! I worship Mother Mud.

THE WILDY ONES

The sheep are in the silver wood,
The cows are in the broom;
The goats are in the wild mountain
And won't be home by noon.

My mother sang that olden tune
Most every night,
And to her newest she would croon
By candle light;
While cuddling in the velvet gloom
I'd dream of cows
That sought each dawn 'mid golden broom
To gently browse.

Or I would glimpse the silver wood,
The birchen glade,
Where pearly sheep in quiet mood
Cropped unafraid;
But how I loved in lapsing drowse
The mountain wild!
The goats were more than sheep and cows
To one wee child.

For cows and sheep are shelter-wise,
    And love the lea;
While goats have starlight in their eyes,
    In cragland free . . .
And now on edge of endless sleep
    Wryly I note
How less I'm kin to kine and sheep
    Than rebel goat!

THE DAUBER

In stilly grove beside the sea
He mingles colours, measures space;
A bronze and breezy man is he,
    Yet peace is in his face.
Behold him stand and longly stare,
Till deft of hand and deep of eye
He captures on a canvas square
    The joy of earth and sky.

Aloof from servitude and strife,
From carking care and greed apart,
Beneath the blue he lives his life
    Of Nature and of Art.
He grieves his pictures must be sold,
Aye, even when his funds are low,
And fat men pay a purse of gold
    He sighs to see them go.

My loving toil is of the pen,
Yet while my verse is not unread,
His pictures will be living when
    My tropes are dim and dead.
God gives us talents great and small,
And though my rhymes I'll never rue,
Sometimes I wish that after all
    I were a dauber too.

FISHERFOLK

I like to look at fishermen
    And oftentimes I wish
One would be lucky now and then
    And catch a little fish.
I watch them statuesquely stand,
    And at the water look;
But if they pull their float to land
    It's just to bait a hook.

I ponder the psychology
    That roots them in their place;
And wonder at the calm I see
    In every angler's face.
There is such patience in their eyes,
    Beside the river's brink;
And waiting for a bite or rise
    I do not think they think.

Or else they are just gentle men,
    Who love—they know not why,
Green grace of trees or water when
    It wimples to the sky . . .
Sweet simple souls! As vain I watch
    My heart to you is kind:
Most precious prize of all you catch,
    —Just Peace of Mind.

KAIL YARD BARD

A very humble pen I ply
  Beneath a cottage thatch;
And in the sunny hours I try
  To till my cabbage patch;
And in the gloaming glad am I
    To lift the latch.

I do not plot to pile up pelf,
  With jowl and belly fat;
To simple song I give myself,
  And seek no gain at that:
Content if milk is on the shelf
    To feed the cat.

I joy that haleness I possess,
  Though fame has passed me by;
And see such gold of happiness
  A-shining in the sky,
I wonder who has won success,
    Proud men or I?

I do not grieve that I am poor,
  And by the world unknown;
Free as the wind, serene and sure,
  In peace I live alone.
'Tis better to be bard obscure
    Than King on Throne.

RHYMES FOR RUE

HER TOYS

I sat her in her baby chair,
    And set upon its tray
Her kewpie doll and teddy bear,
    But no, she would not play.
Although they looked so wistfully
    Her favour to implore,
She laughed at me with elfin glee
    And dashed them to the floor.

I brought her lamb and circus clown,
    But it was just the same:
With shrill of joy she threw them down
    As if it were a game.
Maybe it was, for she would look
    To see where they were lain,
And act pathetic till I took
    Her toys to her again.

To-day there's just an empty chair,
    And 'mid a mist of pain
I'd give my life if she were there
    To toss her toys again.
A tiny ghost is all I see,
    Who laughs the while I cry,
And lifts her little hands with glee
    —Unto the sky.

THE FLOWER SHOP

Because I have no garden and
    No pence to buy,
Before the flower shop I stand
      And sigh.
The beauty of the Springtide spills
    In glowing posies
Of violets and daffodils
      And roses.

And as I see that joy of bloom,
    Sad sighing,
I think of Mother in her room,
    Lone lying.
She babbles of the garden fair
    Her childhood knew,
And how she gathered roses there
      In joyous dew.

I shiver in the street so grey,
    Yet still I stop;
In gutter grime it seems so gay,
    This flower shop . . .
"Oh Mister, could you spare one rose?"
    (There now, I'm crying),
"For Mother,—every blossom knows
      —*Is dying.*"

VAIN VENTURE

To have a business of my own
      With toil and tears,
I wore my fingers to the bone
      For weary years.
With stoic heart, for sordid gold
      In patient pain
My life and liberty I sold
      For others gain.

I scrimped and scraped, as cent by cent
      My savings grew;
I found a faded shop for rent,
      Made it like new.
Above the door the paint was dry
      Where glowed my name:
I waited there for folks to buy—
      But no one came.

Now I am back where I began:
      Myself I sell.
I grovel to a greedy man,
      And life is hell.
An empty shop of bankrupt shame
      I pass before,
Seeing my bitter, bleary name
      Above the door.

THE ANNIVERSARY

"This bunch of violets," he said,
    "Is for my daughter dear.
Since that glad morn when she was wed
    It is today a year.
She lives atop this flight of stairs—
    Please give an arm to me:
If we can take her unawares
    How glad she'll be!"

We climbed the stairs; the flight was four,
    Our steps were stiff and slow;
But as he reached his daughter's door
    His eyes were all aglow.
Joylike he raised his hand to knock,
    Then sore distressed was I,
For from the silence like a shock
    I heard a cry.

A drunken curse, a sob of woe . . .
    His withered face grew grey.
"I think," said he, "we'd better go
    And come another day."
And as he went a block with me,
    Walking with weary feet,
His violets, I sighed to see,
    Bestrewed the street.

TOM

That Tom was poor was sure a pity,
　　Such guts for learning had the lad;
He took to Greek like babe to titty,
　　And he was mathematic mad.
I loved to prime him up with knowledge,
　　A brighter lad I never knew;
I dreamed that he would go to college
　　And there be honoured too.

But no! His Dad said, "Son, I need you
　　To keep the kettle on the boil;
No longer can I clothe and feed you,
　　Buy study books and midnight oil.
I carry on as best I'm able,
　　A humble tailor, as you know;
And you must squat cross-legged a table
　　And learn to snip and sew."

And that is what poor Tom is doing.
　　He bravely makes the best of it;
But as he "fits" you he is knowing
　　That he himself is a misfit;
And thinks as he fulfils his calling,
　　With patient heart yet deep distaste,
Like clippings from his shears down-falling,
　　　　—He, too, is Waste.

THE PORTRAIT

The portrait there above my bed
They tell me is a work of art;
My Wife,—since twenty years she's dead:
Her going nearly broke my heart.
Alas! No little ones we had
To light our hearth with joy and glee;
Yet as I linger lone and sad
    I know she's waiting me.

The picture? Sargent painted it,
And it has starred in many a show.
Her eyes are on me where I sit,
And follow me where'er I go.
She'll smile like that when I am gone,
And I am frail and oh so ill!
Aye, when I'm waxen, cold and wan,
    Lo! She'll be smiling still.

So I have bade them slash in strips
That relic of my paradise.
Let flame destroy those lovely lips
And char the starlight of her eyes!
No human gaze shall ever see
Her beauty,—stranger heart to stir:
Nay, her last smile shall be for me,
    My last look be for her.

KATIE DRUMMOND

My Louis loved me oh so well
    And spiered me for his wife;
He would have haled me from the hell
    That was my bawdy life:
The mother of his bairns to be,
    Daftlike he saw in me.

But I, a hizzie of the town
    Just telt him we must part;
Loving too well to drag him down
    I tore him from my heart:
To save the honour of his name
    I went back to my shame.

They say he soared to starry fame,
    Romance flowed from his pen;
A prince of poets he became,
    Pride of his fellow men:
My breast was pillow for his head,
    Yet naught of his I've read.

Smoking my cutty pipe the while,
    In howths of Leith I lag;
* My Louis lies in South Sea isle
    As I a sodden hag
Live on . . . Oh Love, by men enskied
    The day you went—I died.

* R.L.S.

A YEAR AGO

I'm sitting by the fire tonight,
    The cat purrs on the rug;
The room's abrim with rosy light,
    Suavely soft and snug;
And safe and warm from dark and storm
    It's cosiness I hug.

Then petulant the window pane
    Quakes in the tempest moan,
And cries: "Forlornly in the rain
    There starkly streams a stone,
Where one so dear who shared your cheer
    Now lies alone, alone.

"Go forth! Go forth into the gale
    And pass an hour in prayer;
This night of sorrow do not fail
    The one you deemed so fair,
The girl below the bitter snow
    Who died your child to bear."

So wails the wind, yet here I sit
    Beside the ember's glow;
My grog is hot, my pipe is lit,
    And loth am I to go
To her who died a ten-month bride,
    Only a year ago.

To-day we weep: each morrow is
      A littling of regret;
The saddest part of sorrow is
      That we in time forget . . .
Christ! Let me go to graveyard woe,—
      Yea, I will sorrow yet.

THE SNIPER

Because back home in Tennessee
　　　I was a champeen shot,
They made a sniper outa me
　　　An' ninety krouts I got:
　　　I wish to Christ I'd not!

Athinkin' o' them blasted lives
　　　It's kindo' blue I be;
Them lads no doubt had kids an' wives
　　　An' happy home like me:
　　　Them stiffs I still can see.

Aye, ninety men or more my hand
　　　Has hustled down to hell;
They've loaded me with medals and
　　　They tell me I done well:
　　　A hero for a spell.

But Heaven help me to forget
　　　Them fellow men I've slain,
The bubbling flow of blood I've let . . .
　　　I'll never kill again:
　　　To swat flies gives me pain.

114

Just let me dream when we will see
        And end of soldierin';
When flags of famous victory
        Will be amoulderin':
An' lethal steel an' battle blast
        Be nightmares of the past.

THE WOMAN AT THE GATE

"Where is your little boy to-day?"
   I asked her at the gate.
"I used to see him at his play,
   And often I would wait:
He was so beautiful, so bright,
   I watched him with delight.

"He had a tiny motor-car
   And it was painted red;
He wound it up; it ran so far,
   So merrily it sped.
I think he told me that it was
   A gift from Santa Claus."

The woman said: "It ran so far
   He followed it with joy.
Then came a *real* motor-car,—
   He sought to save his toy . . .
My little boy is far away
   Where angel children play.

"His father perished in the War;
   Now I am all alone,
And death is all I'm longing for . . ."
   So said with face of stone
That woman. "Curse their crazy cars
   And cruel wars!"

ABANDONED DOG

They dumped it on the lonely road,
  Then like a streak they sped;
And as along the way I strode
  I thought that it was dead:
And then I saw that yelping pup
  Rise, race to catch them up.

You know how silly wee dogs are.
  It thought they were in fun.
Trying to overtake their car
  I saw it run and run:
But as they faster, faster went,
  It stumbled, sore and spent.

I found it prone upon the way;
  Of life was little token.
As limply in the dust it lay
  I thought its heart was broken:
Then one dim eye it opened and
  It sought to lick my hand.

Of course I took it gently up
  And brought it to my wife
Who loves all dogs, and now that pup
  Shares in our happy life:
Yet how I curse the bastards who
  Its good luck never knew!

CONVICTS LOVE CANARIES

Dick's dead! It was the Polack guard
Put powdered glass into his cage
When I was tramping round the yard,—
I could have killed him in my rage.
I slugged him with that wrench I stole:
That's why I'm rotting in the Hole.

Dick's dead! Sure I wish I was too.
His honey breast, his lacy claws
I kissed and cried, for well I knew
They murdered him. I cursed because
He was my only chum on earth . . .
Oh how he cheered me with his mirth!

Dick's dead! I know he cared for me.
Being I'm Irish I love song,
And there was heaven in his glee;
I'd bless his heart the dour day long.
I'd let him flutter round the cell;
He'd light upon my hand . . . Oh hell!

Dick's dead! They've thrown me in the Hole.
To break our spirits how they try!
My bed a plank, blind as a mole,
Sure I'll be nuts before I die . . .
Here in the night, dark as the Pit
I'm seeing sunny wings aflit.
Here in the silence, hark his song!
—Poor Dick! Oh Christ, how long, how long!

COMPASSION

A beggar in the street I saw,
Who held a hand like withered claw,
    As cold as clay;
But as I had no silver groat
To give, I buttoned up my coat
    And turned away.

And then I watched a working wife
Who bore the bitter load of life
    With lagging limb;
A penny from her purse she took,
And with sweet pity in her look
    Gave it to him.

Anon I spied a shabby dame
Who fed six sparrows as they came
    In famished flight;
She was so poor and frail and old,
Yet crumbs of her last crust she doled
    With pure delight.

Then sudden in my heart was born
For my sleek self a savage scorn,—
    Urge to atone;
So when a starving cur I saw
I bandaged up its bleeding paw
    And bought a bone.

For God knows it is good to give;
We may not have so long to live,
     So if we can,
Let's do each day a kindly deed,
And stretch a hand to those in need,
     Bird, beast or man.

NO SUNDAY CHICKEN

I could have sold him up because
    His rent was long past due;
And Grimes, my lawyer, said it was
    The proper thing to do:
But how could I be so inhuman?
    And me a gentle-woman.

Yet I am poor as chapel mouse,
    Pinching to make ends meet,
And have to let my little house
    To buy enough to eat:
Why, even now to keep agoing
    I have to take in sewing.

Sylvester is a widowed man,
    Clerk in a hardware store;
I guess he does the best he can
    To feed his kiddies four:
It sure is hard,—don't think it funny,
    I've lately *loaned* him money.

I want to wipe away a tear
    Even to just suppose
Some monster of an auctioneer
    Might sell his sticks and clothes:
I'd rather want for bread and butter
    Than see them in the gutter.

A silly, soft old thing am I,
  But oh them kiddies four!
I guess I'll make a raisin pie
  And leave it at their door . . .
Some Sunday, dears, you'll share my dream,—
  Fried chicken and ice-cream.

THE HEARTH-STONE

The leaves are sick and jaundiced, they
        Drift down the air;
December's sky is sodden grey,
        Dark with despair;
A bleary dawn will light anon
        A world of care.

My name is cut into a stone,
        No care have I;
The letters drool, as I alone
        Forgotten lie:
With weed my grave is overgrown,
        None cometh nigh.

A hundred hollow years will speed
        As I decay;
And I'll be comrade to the weed,
        Kin to the clay;
Until some hind in homing-need
        Will pass my way.

Until some lover seeking hearth
        With joy will see
My nameless stone sunk in the earth
        And it will be
The ruddy birth of childish mirth,
        And elder glee.

And none will dream it bore my name
       Decades ago;
A scribbling fool of little fame,
       Who loved life so . . .
Well, flesh is grass and Time must pass,—
       Heigh ho! Heigh ho!

CHARITY

The Princess was of ancient line,
    Of royal race was she;
Like cameo her face was fine,
    With sad serenity:
Yet bent she toiled with dimming eye,
    Her rice and milk to buy.

With lacework that for pity plead,
    So out of date it seemed,
She sought to make her daily bread,
    As of her past she dreamed:
And though sometimes I heard her sigh,
    I never knew her cry.

Her patient heart was full of hope,
    For health she gave God thanks,
Till one day in an envelope
    I sealed a thousand francs,
And 'neath her door for her to see
    I slipped it secretly.

'Twas long after, I came to know
    My gift she never spent,
But gave to one of greater woe,
    Then wearily she went . . .
To be of charity a part,—
    That stabbed her to the heart.

For one dark day we found her dead:
    Oh she was sweet to see!
Exalted in her garret bed
    With face like ivory . . .
Aye, though from lack of food she died,
    Unflawed she flagged her pride.

CELEBATES

They must not wed the Doctor said,
    For they were far from strong,
And children of their marriage bed
    Might not live overlong.
And yet each eve I saw them pass
    With rapt and eager air,
As fit a seeming lad and lass
        As ought to pair.

For twenty years I went away
    And scoured the China Sea,
Then homing came and found that they
    Were still sweet company.
The Doctor and the Priest had banned
    Three times their wedding ties,
Yet they were walking hand in hand,
        Love in their eyes.

And then I went away again
    For years another score,
And sailored all the Spanish Main
    Ere I returned once more;
And now I see them pass my gate,
    So slow and stooped and grey,
And when I asked them: "Why not mate?"
        "We do," they say.

"No priest and village bells we need,
    No Doctor to approve;
The Lord has wedded us indeed
    With everlasting love.
How wonderful to understand
    The working of His will!
Lo! We are walking hand in hand,
        And sweethearts still."

THE HEALER

"Tuberculosis should not be,"
   The old professor said.
"If folks would hearken unto me
   'Twould save a million dead.
Nay, no consumptive needs to die,
     —A cure have I.

"From blood of turtle I've distilled
     An elixir of worth;
Let every sufferer be thrilled
     And sing for joy of earth;
Yet every doctor turns his back
     And calls me quack.

"Alas! They do not want to cure,
     For sickness is their meat;
So persecution I endure,
     And die in dark defeat:
Ye lungers, listen to my call!
     —I'll save you all."

The old Professor now is dead,
   And turtles of the sea,
Knowing their blood they need not shed,
   Are festive in their glee:
While sanitoriums are crammed
     With legions damned.

WEARY WAITRESS

Her smile ineffably is sweet,
    Divinely she is slim;
Yet oh how weary are her feet,
    How aches her every limb!
Thank God it's near to closing time,
    —Merciful midnight chime.

Then in her mackintosh she'll go
    Up seven flights of stairs,
And on her bed her body throw,
    Too tired to say her prayers;
Yet not too sleepy to forget
    Her cheap alarm to set.

She dreams . . . That lonely bank-clerk boy
    Who comes each day for tea,—
Oh how his eyes light up with joy
    Her comeliness to see!
And yet he is too shy to speak,
    Far less to touch her cheek.

He dreams . . . If only I were King
    I'd make of her my Queen.
If I were laureate I'd sing
    Her loveliness serene.
—How wistfully romance can haunt
    A city restaurant!

For as I watch that pensive pair
    There stirs within my heart
From Arcady an April air
    That shames the sordid mart:
A sense of Spring and singing rills,
    —Love mid the daffodils.

ARMISTICE DAY (1953)

Don't jeer because we celebrate
        Armistice Day,
Though thirty years of sorry fate
        Have passed away.
Though still we guard the Sacred Flame,
        And fly the Flag,
That World War Two with grief and shame
        Revealed—a rag.

For France cannot defend to-day
        Her native land;
And she is far too proud to pray
        For helping hand.
Aye, though she stands amid the Free,
        In love with life,
No more her soil will shambles be
        In world-war strife.

Still we who tend the deathless Flame
        Of Verdun speak;
It is our glory and our shame,
        For we are weak.
We have too much of blood and blight
        To answer for . . .
No, France will never, never fight
        Another war!

A PLEA

Why need we newer arms invent,
  Poor peoples to destroy?
With what we have let's be content
  And perfect their employ.
With weapons that may millions kill,
  Why should we seek for more,
A brighter spate of blood to spill,
  A deeper sea of gore?

The lurid blaze of atom light
  Vast continents will blind,
And steep in centuries of night
  Despairing humankind.
So let's be glad for gun and blade,
  To fight with honest stuff:
Are tank, block-buster, hand-grenade
  And napalm not enough?

Oh to go back a thousand years
  When arrows winged their way,
When foemen fell upon the spears
  And swords were swung to slay!
Behold! Belching in Heaven black
  Mushrooms obscene!
Dear God, the brave days give us back,
  When wars were clean!

THE MONSTER

When we might make with happy heart
    This world a paradise,
With bombs we blast brave men apart,
    With napalm carbonize.
Where we might till the sunny soil,
    And sing for joy of life,
We spend our treasure and our toil
      In bloody strife.

The fields of wheat are sheening gold,
    The flocks have silver fleece;
The signs are sweetly manifold
    Of plenty, praise and peace.
Yet see! The sky is like a cowl
    Where grimy toilers bore
The shards of steel that feed the foul
      Red maw of War.

Instead of butter give us guns;
    Instead of sugar, shells.
Devoted mothers, bear your sons
    To glut still hotter hells.
Alas! When will mad mankind wake
    To banish evermore,
And damn for God in Heaven's sake
      Mass Murder—WAR?

RHYMES FOR REVERENCE

AGNOSTIC

The chapel looms against the sky,
 Above the vine-clad shelves,
And as the peasants pass it by
 They cross themselves.
But I alone, I grieve to state,
 Lack sentiment divine:
A citified sophisticate,
 I make no sign.

Their gesture may a habit be,
 Mechanic in a sense,
Yet somehow it awakes in me
 Strange reverence.
And though from ignorance it stem,
 Somehow I deeply grieve,
And wish down in my heart like them
 I could believe.

Suppose a cottage I should buy,
 And little patch of vine,
With pure and humble spirit I
 Might make the Sign.
Aye, though a godless way I go,
 And sceptic is my trend,
A faith in *something I don't know*
 Might save me in the end.

MY CHILDHOOD GOD

When I was small the Lord appeared
        Unto my mental eye
A gentle giant with a beard
        Who homed up in the sky.
But soon that vasty vision blurred,
        And faded in the end,
Till God is just another word
        I cannot comprehend.

I envy those of simple faith
        Who bend the votive knee;
Who do not doubt divinely death
        Will set their spirits free.
Oh could I be like you and you,
        Sweet souls who scan this line,
And by dim altar worship too
        A Deity Divine!

Alas! Mid passions that appal
        I ask with bitter woe
Is God responsible for all
        Our horror here below?
He made the hero and the saint,
        But did He also make
The cannibal in battle paint,
        The shark and rattlesnake?

If I believe in God I should
    Believe in Satan too;
The one the source of all our good,
    The other of our rue . . .
Oh could I second childhood gain!
    For then it might be, I
Once more would see that vision plain,—
    Fond Father in the sky.

THE HOST

I never could imagine God:
I don't suppose I ever will.
Beside His altar fire I nod
With senile drowsiness but still
In old of age as sight grows dim
      I have a sense of Him.

For when I count my sum of days
I find so many sweet and good,
My mind is full of peace and praise,
My heart aglow with gratitude.
For my long living in the sun
      I want to *thank* someone.

Someone who has been kind to me;
Some power within, if not on high,
Who shaped my gentle destiny,
And led me pleasant pastures by:
Who taught me, whether gay or grave,
      To love the life He gave.

A Host of charity and cheer,
Within a Tavern warm and bright;
Who smiles and bids me have no fear
As forth I fare into the night:
From whom I beg no Heav'n, but bless
      For *earthly* happiness.

GOD'S VAGABOND

A passion to be free
Has ever mastered me;
To none beneath the sun
Will I bow down,—not one
Shall leash my liberty.

My life's my own; I rise
With glory in my eyes;
And my concept of hell
Is to be forced to sell
Myself to one who buys.

With heart of rebel I
Man's government defy;
With hate of bondage born
Monarch and mob I scorn:
My King the Lord on high.

God's majesty I know;
And worship in the glow
Of beauty that I see,
Of love embracing me;
My heaven to be free:
May it be ever so.

LORD LET ME LIVE

Lord, let me live, that more and more
    Your wonder world I may adore;
With every dawn to grow and grow
    Alive to graciousness aglow;
And every eve in beauty see
        Reason for rhapsody.

Lord, let me bide, that I may prove
    The buoyant brightness of my love
For sapphire sea and lyric sky
    And buttercup and butterfly;
And glory in the golden thought
        Of rapture You have wrought.

Lord, let me linger, just for this,—
    To win to utterness of bliss;
To see in every dawn design
    Proof of Your Providence divine;
With night to find ablaze above,
        Assurance of Your love.

Lord, for Your praise my days prolong,
    That I may sing in sunny sort,
And prove with my exultant song
    The longest life is all too short:
Aye, even in a bead of dew
        To shrine in beauty—YOU.

THE TRUST

Because I've eighty years and odd,
    And darkling is my day,
I now prepare to meet my God,
    And for forgiveness pray.
Not for salvation is my plea,
    Nor Heaven hope,—just rest:
Begging: "Dear Father, pardon me,
    I did not do my best.

"I did not measure with the Just
    To serve my fellow men;
But unto levity and lust
    I loaned my precious pen.
I sorrow for the sacred touch,
    And though I toiled with zest,
Dear God, have mercy, in-as-much
    I did not do my best.

"I bless You for the gift you gave
    That brought me golden joy;
Yet here beside the gentle grave
    I grieve for its employ.
Have pity, Lord,—so well I know
    I failed you in the test,
And my last thought is one of woe:
    I did not do my best."

A RUSTY NAIL

I ran a nail into my hand,
   The wound was hard to heal;
So bitter was the pain to stand
   I thought how it would feel,
To have spikes thrust through hands and feet,
   Impaled by hammer beat.

Then hoisted on a cross of oak
   Against the sullen sky,
With all about the jeering folk
   Who joyed to see me die;
Die hardly in insensate heat,
   With bleeding hands and feet.

Yet was it not that day of Fate,
   Of cruelty insane,
Climaxing centuries of hate
   That woke our souls to pain!
And are we not the living seed
   Of those who did the deed!

Of course, with thankful heart I know
   We are not fiends as then;
And in a thousand years or so
   We may be *gentle* men.
But it has cost a poisoned hand,
   And pain beyond a cry,
To make me strangely understand
   A Cross against the sky.

OMMISSION

What man has not betrayed
    Some sacred trust?
If haply you are made
    Of honest dust,
Vaunt not of glory due,
    Of triumph won:
Think, think of duties you
    Have left undone.

But if in mercy hope,
    Despite your sin,
The gates of Heaven ope'
    To let you in:
Pray, pray that when God reads
    Your judgement due,
He may forget good deeds
    You did not do.

Ommission sins may be
    The bitterest,
And wring in memory
    A heart opprest;
So when sweet pity pleads,
    Let us not rue
Too late, too late Kind Deeds
    We did not do.

PRAGMATIC

When young I was an Atheist,
      Yea, pompous as a pigeon
No opportunity I missed
      To satirize religion.
I sneered at Scripture, scoffed at Faith,
      I blasphemed at believers:
Said I: "There's nothing after Death,—
      Your priests are just deceivers."

In middle age I was not so
      Contemptuous and caustic.
Thought I: "There's much I do not know:
      I'd better be agnostic.
The hope of immortality
      'Tis foolish to be flouting."
So in the end I came to be
      A doubter of my doubting.

Now I am old, with steps inclined
      To hesitate and falter;
I find I get such peace of mind
      Just sitting by an altar.
So Friends, don't scorn the family pew,
      The preachments of the kirks:
Religion may be false or true,
      But by the Lord!—it works.

146

A GRAIN OF SAND

If starry space no limit knows
    And sun succeeds to sun,
There is no reason to suppose
    Our earth the only one.
'Mid countless constellations cast
    A million worlds may be,
With each a God to bless or blast
    And steer to destiny.

Just think! A million gods or so
    To guide each vital stream,
With over all to boss the show
    A Deity supreme.
Such magnitudes oppress my mind;
    From cosmic space it swings;
So ultimately glad to find
    Relief in little things.

For look! Within my hollow hand,
    While round the earth careens,
I hold a single grain of sand
    And wonder what it means.
Ah! If I had the eyes to see,
    And brain to understand,
I think Life's mystery might be
    Solved in this grain of sand.

DIVINE DEVICE

Would it be loss or gain
To hapless human-kind
If we could feel no pain
Of body or of mind?
Would it be for our good
If we were calloused so,
And God in mercy should
End all our woe?

I wonder and I doubt:
It is my bright belief
We should be poor without
The gift of grief.
For suffering may be
A blessing, not a bane,
And though we sorrow we
Should praise for Pain.

Aye, it's my brave belief
That grateful we should be,
Since in the heart of grief
Is love and sympathy.
We do not weep in vain,
So let us kiss the rod,
And see in purging Pain
The Grace of God.

GOD'S GRIEF

"Lord God of Hosts," the people pray,
"Make strong our arms that we may slay
Our cursed foe and win the day."
"Lord God of Battles," cries the foe,
"Guide us to strike a bloody blow,
And lay the adversary low."

But brooding o'er the battle smother
Bewails the Lord: "Brother to brother,
Why must ye slaughter one another?
When will ye come to understand
My peace, and hand reach out to hand,
In every race, in every land?"

And yet, his weary words despite,
Went murderously on the fight,
Till God from mankind hid His sight,
Saying: "Poor children, must you gain
To brotherhood through millions slain?
—Was anguish on the Cross in vain?"

DESIGN

Said Seeker of the skies to me:
"Behold yon starry host ashine!
When Heaven's harmony you see
How can you doubt control divine,
       Law, order and design?"

"Nay, Sire," said I, "I do not doubt
The spheres in cosmic pattern spin;
But what I try to puzzle out
Is that—if Law and Order win
       Where does mere man come in?

"If to the millionth of a hair
Cause and Effect are welded true,
Then there's no leeway anywhere,
And all we do we *have* to do,
       And sun and atom too."

O Stars, sing in your harmony!
O Constellations raptly shine!
Flout me because I am not free,
Mock me because no choice is mine!
O Beauty, it so hurts to see!
       —O damnable Design!

RELATIVITY

I looked down on a daisied lawn
To where a host of tiny eyes
Of snow and gold from velvet shone
And made me think of starry skies.

I looked up to the vasty night
Where stars were very small indeed,
And in their galaxy of light
They made me think of daisied mead.

I took a daisy in my hold;
Its snowy rays were tipped with rose,
And with its tiny boss of gold
I thought—how like a star it glows!

I dreamt I plucked from Heaven's field
A star and held it in my hand.
Said I: "The might of God I wield,
The Great and Small I understand."

For when the All is said and done,
In Time and Space I seem to see
A daisy equal to a sun,
Between heart-beats—Eternity.

MIRACLES

Each time that I switch on the light
A Miracle it seems to me
That I should rediscover sight
And banish dark so utterly.
One moment I am bleakly blind,
The next—exultant life I find.

Below the sable of the sky
My eyelids double darkness make.
Sleep is divine, yet oh how I
Am glad with wonder to awake!
To welcome, glimmery and wan
The mighty Miracle of Dawn.

For I've mad moments when I seem,
With all the marvel of a child,
To dwell within a world of dream,
To sober fact unreconciled.
Each simple act has struck me thus—
Incredibly miraculous.

When everything I see and do
So magical can seem to me,
How vain it is to seek the True,
The riddle of Reality . . .
So let me with joy lyrical
Proclaim all Life a Miracle!

THE LAW OF LAWS

If we could roll back History
    A century, let's say,
And start from there, I'm sure that we
    Would find things as to-day:
In all creation's cosmic range
    No vestige of a change.

Turn back a thousand years, the same
    Unchangement we would view;
Cause and Effect their laws proclaim,
    The truest of the true,
And in life's mechanistic groove
    The Universe would move.

Grim is the grip of the Machine
    And everything we do
Designed implacably has been
    Since earth was virgin new:
We strut our parts as they were writ,—
    That's all there is to it.

Curse on such thinking! Let us play
    At Free Will, though we be
The gnatlike creatures of a day,
    The dupes of Destiny . . .
The merle is merry in the may—
    Tomorrow's time to pray.

THE SCORE

Because I've come to eighty odd,
I must prepare to meet you, God.
What should I do? I cannot pray,
I have no pious words to say;
And though the Bible I might read,
      Scriptures don't meet my need.

Please tell me God what can I do
To be acceptable to you?
I've put in order my affairs,
And left their portion to my heirs;
And what remains I've willed to be
      A gift to Charity.

What must I do? I cannot kneel,
Although a sense of you I feel,
I will not show a coward's fear,
Waiting until the end be near
To pester you with mercy plea,
      —You'd be despising me.

I hope I have been kind and true;
I've helped to happiness a few.
I've made a mother's eye to smile,
I've played with little ones a while.
I do not know what is the score;
Of good I might have done much more:
But now I guess my exit's due;—
    Dear God, it's up to You!

FOOL FAITH

Said I: "See yon vast heaven shine,—
    What earthly sight diviner?
Before such radiant Design
    Why doubt Designer?"

Said he: "Design is just a thought
    In human cerebration,
And meaningless if Man is not
    Part of creation.

"But grant Design,—we may imply
    The job took toil aplenty;
Then why one sole designer, why
    Not ten or twenty.

"But should there be *one* Source supreme
    Of matter and of motion,
Why mould it like our man-machine
    For daft devotion?"

Said I: "You may be right or wrong,
    I'll seek not to discover . . .
I listen to yon starry song,—
    Still, still God's lover."

DARK TRINITY

Said I to Pain: "You would not dare
        Do ill to me."
Said Pain: "Poor fool! Why should I care
        Whom you may be?
To clown and king alike I bring
        My meed of bane;
Why should you shirk my chastening?"
           Said Pain.

Said I to Grief: "No tears have I,
        Go on your way."
Said Grief: "Why should I pass you by,
        While others pay?
All men must know the way of woe,
        From saint to thief,
And tears were meant to overflow,"
           Said Grief.

Said I to Death: "From ail and fret
        Grant me relief."
Said Death: "I know you are beset
        By Pain and Grief.
But my good will you must await
        Since human breath
To suffering is consecrate,"
           Said Death.

Said I to God: "Pale Sister Grief,
        Bleak Brother Pain,
Bedevil me beyond belief,
        And Death's unfain . . ."
Said God: "Curse not that blessed Three,
        Poor human clod!
Have faith! Believe them *One with Me,*"
        Said God.

RHYMES FOR REST

EYRIE

Between the mountain and the sea
    I've made a happy landing;
And here a peace has come to me
    That passeth understanding;
A shining faith and purity
    Beyond demanding.

With palm below and pine above,
    Where wings of gulls are gleaming;
By orange tree and olive grove,
    From walls of airy seeming,
My roses beg me not to rove,
    But linger dreaming.

So I'm in love with life again,
    And would with joy dissever
My days from ways of worldly men,
    And mingle with them never:
Let silken roses to my ken
    Whisper forever.

I SHALL NOT BURN

I have done with love and lust,
　　I reck not for gold or fame;
I await familiar dust
　　These frail fingers to reclaim:
　　Not for me the tiger flame.

Not for me the furnace glow,
　　Rage of fire and ashen doom;
To sweet earth my bones bestow
　　Where above a lowly tomb
　　January roses bloom.

Fools and fools and fools are you
　　Who your dears to fires confide;
Give to Mother Earth her due:
　　Flesh may waste but bone will bide,—
　　Let loved ones lie side by side.

Let God's Acre ever dream;
　　Shed your tears and blossoms bring;
On age-burnished bone will gleam
　　Crucifix and wedding ring:
　　Graves are for sweet comforting.

　　Curst be those who my remains
　　Hurl to horror of the flames!

SIX FEET OF SOD

This is the end of all my ways,
    My wanderings on earth,
My gloomy and my golden days,
    My madness and my mirth.
I've bought ten thousand blades of grass
    To bed me down below,
And here I wait the days to pass
        Until I go

Until I bid good bye to friend,
    To feast and fast goodbye,
And in a stint of soil the end
    I seek of sun and sky.
My farings far on land and sea,
    My trails of global girth
Sum up to this,—to cover me
        Six feet of earth.

My home of homes I hold in fee
    For centuries to pass,
When snug my skeleton will be
    And grin up through the grass;
When my grey ghost will bend above,
    And grieve to gracious God
This endless end of life and love,—
        Six feet of sod.

EPITAPH

No matter how he toil and strive
The fate of every man alive
With luck will be to lie alone,
His empty name cut in a stone.

Grim time the fairest fame will flout,
But though his name be blotted out,
And he forgotten with his peers,
His stone may wear a year of years.

No matter how we sow and reap
The end of all is endless sleep;
From strife a merciful release,
From life the crowning prize of Peace.

COURAGE

In the shadow of the grave
    I will be brave;
I'll smile,—I know I will
    E'er I be still;
Because I will not smile
    So long a while.

But I'll be sad, I fear,
    And shed a tear,
For those I love and leave
    My loss to grieve:
'Tis just their grief I'll grieve,
    Believe, believe.

Not for myself I care
    As forth I fare;
But for those left behind
    Wae is my mind;
Knowing how they will miss
    My careless kiss.

Oh I'll be brave when I
    Shall come to die;
With courage I will quaff
    The Cup and laugh,
Aye, even mock at Death
    With failing breath.

It is not those who go
      Who suffer woe;
But stricken ones who bide
      By cold bedside:
God comfort you who keep
      Watch by my sleep!

MY CALENDAR

From off my calendar today
    A leaf I tear;
So swiftly passes smiling May
    Without a care.
And now the gentleness of June
    Will fleetly fly
And I will greet the glamour moon
    Of lush July.

Beloved months so soon to pass,
    Alas, I see
The slim sand silvering the glass
    Of Time for me;
As bodingly midwinter woe
    I wait with rue,
Oh how I grudge the days to go!
    They are so few.

A Calendar's a gayful thing
    To grace a room;
And though with joy of life I sing,
    With secret gloom
I add this merry month of May
    To eighty past,
Thinking each page I tear away
    May be my last.

HUMILITY

My virtues in Carara stone
Cut carefully you all may scan;
Beneath I lie, a fetid bone,
The marble worth more than the man.

If on my pure tomb they should grave
My vices,—how the folks would grin!
And say with sympathetic wave:
"Like us he was a man of sin."

And somehow he consoled thereby,
Knowing they may, though Hades bent,
When finally they come to die,
Enjoy a snow-white monument.

And maybe it is just as well
When we from life and lust are riven,
That though our souls should sink to hell
Our tombs point: *Destination Heaven!*

I WILL NOT FIGHT

I will not fight: though proud of pith
I hold no one worth striving with;
And should resentment burn my breast
I deem that silence serves me best:
So having not a word to say,
Contemptuous I turn away.

I will not fret: my rest of life
Free I will keep from hate and strife;
Let lust and sin and anger sleep,
I will not delve the subsoil deep,
But be content with inch of earth,
Where daisies have their birth.

I will not grieve: Till day be done
I will be tranquil in the sun,
With garden glow and quiet nook,
And song of bird and spell of book . . .
God bless you all! I will not fight,
But love and dream until—Goodnight!

EVENFALL

When day is done I steal away
    To fold my hands in rest,
And of my hours this moment grey
        I love the best;
So quietly I sit alone
    And wait for evenfall,
When in the dusk doves sweetly moan
        And crickets call.

With heart of humble gratitude
    How it is good to bide,
And know the joy of solitude
        In eventide!
When one is slow and slips a bit,
    And life begins to pall,
How sweet it is in peace to sit
        At evenfall!

I play upon a simple lute,
    My notes are faint and few,
But ere my melodies be mute,
        Pray one be true.
Lord, let the theme be thankfulness!
    And as I wait my call,
More than noon rapture let me bless
        Life's evenfall!

THE DEFEATED

Think not because you raise
  A gleaming sword,
That you will win to praise
  Before the Lord.

And though men hail you great
  Unto the skies,
Deem not 'twill ope' the gate
  Of Paradise.

Though you have gold and gear
  And fame and power,
What odds when you draw near
  The Judgement Hour?

But if in bloody dust
  Yet unafraid
You battle for the Just
  With broken blade—

Then will the Lord look down
  With eyes of love,
And you shall win a Crown
  All price above.

INDIFFERENCE

When I am dead I will not care
      Forever more,
If sky be radiantly fair
      Or tempest roar.
If my life-hoard in sin be spent,
      My wife re-wed,—
I'll be so damned indifferent
      When I am dead.

When I meet up with dusty doom
      What if I rest
In common ditch or marble tomb,
      If curst or blest?
Shall my seed be to wealth or fame,
      Or gallows led,—
To me it will be all the same
      When I am dead.

So say for me no pious prayer,
      Be no tear shed;
In nothingness I cannot care,
      I'll be so dead.
I shall not reck of war or peace .
      When I go hence:
Lord, let me win sublime release,—
      INDIFFERENCE!

SINISTER SOOTH

You say I am the slave of Fate
Bound by unalterable laws.
I harken, but your words I hate,
Your damnable Effect and Cause.
If there's no hope for happy Chance
Give me the bliss of ignorance.

You say my life ends with the tomb;
This brain, my mind machine, will rot;
Its many million cells that room
My personality and thought
Will in the Dark Destroyer's term
Provide a banquet for the worm.

You say—yet though your wisdom wells,
To it I am unreconciled;
My mind admits, my heart rebels . . .
O let me listen like a child
To Him who spoke with blessed breath
From bench of toil in Nazareth!

THE TRAIL OF NO RETURN

So now I take a bitter road
  Whereon no bourne I see,
And wearily I lift the load
  That once I bore with glee.
For me no more by sea or shore
  Adventure's star shall burn,
As I forsake wild ways to take
  The Trail of No Return.

Such paths of peril I have trod:
  In sun and shade they lay.
And some went wistfully to God,
  And some the devil's way.
But there is one I may not shun,
  Though long my life's sojourn:
A dawn will break when I must take
  The Trail of No Return.

Farewell to friends, good-bye to foes,
  Adieu to smile or frown;
My voyaging is nigh its close,
  And dark is drifting down.
With weary feet my way I beat,
  Yet holy light discern . . .
So let me take without heart-break
  The Trail of No Return.

PROPERTY

The red-roofed house of dream design
    Looks three ways on the sea;
For fifty years I've made it mine,
    And held it part of me.
The pines I planted in my youth
    Triumphantly are tall . . .
Yet now I know with sorry sooth
    I have to leave it all.

Hard-hewn from out the living rock
    And salty from the tide,
My house has braved the tempest shock
    With hardihood and pride.
Each nook is memoried to me;
    I've loved its every stone,
And cried to it exultantly:
    "My own, my very own!"

Poor fool! To think that I *possess.*
    I have but cannot hold;
And all that's mine is less and less
    My own as I grow old.
My home shall ring with childish cheers
    When I shall leave it lone;
My house will bide a hundred years
    When I am in the bone.

Alas! No thing can be my own:
    At most a life-long lease
Is all I hold, a little loan
    From Time, that soon will cease.
For now by faint and failing breath
    I feel that I must go . . .
Old House! You've never known a death,—
    Well, now's your hour to know.

BELATED BARD

The songs I made from joy of earth
      In wanton wandering,
Are rapturous with Maytime mirth
      And ecstasy of Spring.
But all the songs I sing today
      Take tediously the ear:
Novemberishly dark are they
      With mortuary fear.

For half a century has gone
      Since first I rang a rhyme;
And that is long to linger on
      The tolerance of Time.
This blue-veined hand with which I write
      Yet answers to my will;
Though four-score years I count to-night
      I am unsilent still.

"Senile old fool!" I hear you say;
      "Beside the dying fire
You huddle and stiff-fingered play
      Your tired and tinny lyre."
Well, though your patience I may try,
      Bear with me yet awhile,
And though you scorn my singing I
      Will thank you with a smile.

For I such soul-delighting joy
    Have found in simple rhyme,
Since first a happy-hearted boy
    I coaxed a word to chime,
That ere I tryst with Mother Earth
    Let from my heart arise
A song of youth and starry mirth . . .
    Then close my eyes.

LEAVES

The leaves are falling one and one,
    Each like a life to me,
As over-soonly in the sun
    They spiral goldenly:
So airily and warily
    They falter free.

The leaves are falling two and two,
    Beneath a baleful sky;
So silently the sward they strew,
    Reluctantly they die . . .
Rich crimson leaves,—and no one grieves
    Their doom but I.

The leaves are falling three and three
    Beneath the mothlike moon;
They flutter downward silverly
    In muted rigadoon;
And russet dry remote they lie
    From feathered tune.

The leaves are lying numberless,
    Disconsolately dead;
Where lucent was their sylvan dress
    And lightsome was their tread,
They rot below the bitter snow,
    Uncomforted.

A leaf's a life, and one by one
        They drift each darkling day;
Rare friends who lusted in the sun
        Are frailing fast away . . .
How sadly soon will mourn the moon
        My dark decay!

FULFILMENT

I sing of starry dreams come true,
    Of hopes fulfilled;
Of rich reward beyond my due,
    Of harvest milled.
The full fruition of the years
    Is mine to hold,
And in despite of toil and tears
    The sun is gold.

I have no hate for any one
    On this good earth;
My days of hardihood are done,
    And hushed my hearth.
No echo of a world afar
    Can trouble me;
Above a grove the evening star
    Serene I see.

No jealousy nor passion base
    Can irk me now;
Received am I unto God's grace
    With tranquil brow.
Adieu to love I have and hold,
    Farewell to friend;
In peace and faith my hands I fold
    And wait the end.

RHYME BUILDER

I envy not those gay galoots
Who count on dying in their boots;
For that, to tell the sober truth
Should be the privilege of youth;
But aged bones are better sped
To heaven from a downy bed.

So prop me up with pillows two,
And serve me with the barley brew;
And put a pencil in my hand,
A copy book at my command;
And let my final effort be
To ring a rhyme of homely glee.

For since I've loved it oh so long,
Let my last labour be in song;
And when my pencil falters down,
Oh may a final couplet crown
The years of striving I have made
To justify the jinglers trade.

Let me surrender with a rhyme
My long and lovely lease of time;
Let me be grateful for the gift
To couple words in lyric lift;
Let me song-build with humble hod,
My last brick dedicate to God.

MY WILL

I've made my Will. I don't believe
      In luxury and wealth;
And to those loving ones who grieve
      My age and frailing health
I give the meed to soothe their ways
      That they may happy be,
And pass serenely all their days
      In snug security.

That duty done, I leave behind
      The all I have to give
To crippled children and the blind
      Who lamentably live;
Hoping my withered hand may freight
      To happiness a few
Poor innocents whom cruel fate
      Has cheated of their due.

I am no grey philanthropist,
      Too humble is my lot
Yet how I'm glad to give the grist
      My singing mill has brought.
For I have had such lyric days,
      So rich, so full, so sweet,
That I with gratitude and praise
      Would make my life complete.

I'VE MADE MY WILL: now near the end,
       At peace with all mankind,
To children lame I would be friend,
       And brother to the blind . . .
And if there be a God, I pray
       He bless my last bequest,
And in His love and pity say:
       "Good servant,—rest!"

L'ENVOI

Ever in the ebb and flow
Of my dreams that come and go,
Reader, I have you in mind,
Humbly hoping you will find
In my verse a gleam that's true
To the dreams that live in you.

Though my lines I link with rhyme
I scarce deem them worth a dime;
Nay, I think 'tis I who ought
To repay your kindly thought,
Gleaning in the words I waste
One or two to fit your taste.

Please you, lift this little book,
Riffle it with careless look;
Dip in it,—oh just a glance,
Give a beggar bard a chance . . .
Rhymers may have readers who
Tune to them,—may one be you!

RHYMES FOR
MY RAGS

SONGS OF A GRAND-SIRE

PRELUDE

Because the rhymes I make for raiment
Fail to avail its meed of payment,
I fain must make my well-worn tweeds
Suffice me for tomorrow's needs—
Until my verse the public reads.

I used to go to Savile Row,
But now their prices are so high,
With royalties at all time low,
Because my books few want to buy . . .
No, I don't blame them, but that's why.

Well, anyway I'd rather fare
In tattered rags and ring my chimes
Than strut around in wealthy wear.
—So in these tough and trying times
Let me flaunt like defiant flags
The jubilation of my RAGS.

OLD CODGER

Of garden truck he made his fare,
    As his bright eyes bore witness;
Health was his habit and his care,
    His hobby human fitness.
He sang the praise of open sky,
    The gladth of Nature's giving;
And when at last he came to die
    It was of too long living.

He held aloof from hate and strife,
    Drank peace in dreamful doses;
He never voted in his life,
    Loved children, dogs and roses.
Let tyrants romp in gory glee,
    And revolutions roister,
He passed his days as peacefully
    As friar in a cloister.

So fellow sinners, should you choose
    Of doom to be a dodger,
At eighty be a bland recluse
    Like this serene old codger,
Who turned his back on fear and fret,
    And died nigh eighty-seven . . .
His name was—Robert Service: let
    Us hope he went to Heaven.

MAMMY

I often wonder how
    Life clicks because
They don't make women now
    Like Mammy was.
When broods of two or three
    Content most men,
How wonderful was she
    With children ten!

Though sixty years have gone,
    As I look back,
I see her rise at dawn,
    Our boots to black;
Pull us from drowsy bed,
    Wet sponge to pass,
And speed us porridge fed
    To morning class.

Our duds to make and mend,
    Far into night,
O'er needle she would spend
    By bleary light.
Yet as her head drooped low,
    With withered hair,
It seemed the candle glow
    Made halo there.

And so with silvered pow
    I sigh because
They don't make women now
    Like Mammy was.

LINDY LOU

If the good King only knew,
        Lindy Lou,
What a cherub child are you,
        It is true,
He would step down from his throne,
And would claim you for his own,
Then whatever would I do,
        Lindy Lou?

As I kiss your tiny feet,
        Lindy Lou,
I just feel I want to eat
        All of you.
What's so heaven-sweet and mild
As a happy baby-child?
If you died I would die too,
        Lindy Lou.

What's so lovely on this earth,
        Lindy Lou,
As your innocence and mirth
        Shining through?
Let us all do what we may
To make little children gay,
Heaven-happy, just as you,
        Lindy Lou.

THE OLD GENERAL

Little Annabelle to please,
    (Lacking grace, I grant),
Grandpa down on hands and knees
    Plays the elephant.
Annabelle shrieks with delight,
    Bouncing up and down,
On his back and holding tight
    To his dressing gown.

As they roll and bowl along,
    Round and round the room,
There is sunshine and a song
    'Spite December gloom.
Yet we hear not Grandpa's groans,
    Hushed his beard inside,
As his old rheumatic bones
    Ache with every stride.

He has known his golden days,
    Soldiered with the best;
And to prove the people's praise
    Medals bright his breast.
Yet though his renown we chant,
    How we love him well
When he plays the elephant
    Just for Annabelle!

MISS MISCHIEVOUS

Miss Don't-do-this and Don't-do-that
        Has such a sunny smile
You cannot help but chuckle at
        Her cuteness and her guile.
Her locks are silken floss of gold,
        Her eyes are pansy blue:
Maybe of years to eighty old
        The best is two.

Miss Don't-do-this and Don't-do-that
        To roguishness is fain;
To guard that laughter-loving brat
        Is quite a strain;
But when she tires of prank and play
        And says good-night,
I'm longing for another day
        Of child delight.

Miss Don't-do-this and Don't-do-that
        Will grow up soon.
I hope she'll never throw her hat
        Athwart the moon.
Yet I'll be sorrowful indeed,
        Remembering a day
Before she learned to humbly heed
        The word OBEY.

BALLOON

I bought my little grandchild Ann
    A bright balloon,
And I was such a happy man
    To hear her croon.
She laughed and babbled with delight,
    So gold its glow,
As by a thread she held it tight,
    Then—let it go.

As if it gloried to be free
    It climbed the sky;
But oh how sorrowful was she,
    And sad was I!
And when at eve with sobbing cry
    She saw the moon,
She pleaded to the pensive sky
    For her balloon.

O Little One, I pray that you
    In years to be,
Will hold a tiny baby too,
    And know its glee;
That yours will always be the thrill
    And joy of June,
And that you never, never will
    Cry for the moon.

SUSIE

My daughter Susie, aged two,
  Apes me in every way,
For as my household chores I do
  With brooms she loves to play.
A scrubbing brush to her is dear;
  Ah! Though my soul it vex,
My bunch of cuteness has, I fear,
    Kitchen complex.

My dream was that she might go far,
  And play or sing or dance;
Aye, even be a movie star
  Of glamour and romance.
But no more with such hope I think,
  For now her fondest wish is
To draw a chair up to the sink
    And wash the dishes.

Yet when you put it to a test
  In ups and downs of life,
A maiden's mission may be best
  To make a good house-wife;
To bake, to cook, to knit, to lave:
  And so I pray that Sue
Will keep a happy hearth and have
    A baby too.

YOUNG MOTHER

Her baby was so full of glee,
      And through the day
It laughed and babbled on her knee
      In happy play.
It pulled her hair all out of curl
      With noisy joy;
So peppy she was glad her girl
      Was not a boy.

Then as she longed for it to sleep,
      To her surprise
It just relaxed within her keep
      With closing eyes.
And as it lay upon her breast
      So still its breath,
So exquisite its utter rest
      It looked like death.

It seemed like it had slipped away
      To shadow land;
With tiny face like tinted clay
      And waxen hand.
No ghost of sigh, no living look . . .
      Then with an ache
Of panic fear and love she shook
      Her babe awake.

NATURE'S TOUCH

In kindergarten classed
      Dislike they knew;
And as the years went past
      It grew and grew;
Until in maidenhood
      Each sought a mate,
Then venom in their mood
      Was almost hate.

The lure of love they learned
      And they were wed;
Yet when they met each turned
      Away a head;
Each went her waspish way
      With muted damns—
Until they met one day
      With baby prams.

Then lo! Away was swept
      The scorn of years;
Hands clasped they almost wept
      With gentle tears.
Forgetting hateful days,
      All mother mild,
Each took with tender praise
      The other's child.

And now they talk of milk,
  Of diapers and such;
Of baby bosoms silk
  And tender to the touch.
A gemlike girl and boy,—
  With hope unsaid,
Each thinks with mother joy:
  'May these two wed!'

STRIP TEASER

My precious grand-child, aged two,
Is eager to unlace one shoe,
      And then the other;
Her cotton socks she'll deftly doff,
Despite the mild reproaches of
      Her mother.

Around the house she loves to fare,
And with her rosy tootsies bare,
      Pit-pat the floor;
And though remonstrances we make
She presently decides to take
      Off something more.

Her pinafore she next unties,
And then before we realise,
      Her dress drops down;
Her panties and her *brassiere,*
Her chemise and her underwear
      Are round her strown.

And now she dances all about,
As naked as a new-caught trout,
      With impish glee;
And though she's beautiful like that,
(A cherubim, but not so fat),
      Quite shocked are we.

And so we dread with dim dismay
Some day she may her charms display
     In skimpy wear;
Aye, even in a gee-string she
May frolic on the stage of the
     Folies-Bèrgere.

But e'er she does, I hope she'll read
This worldly wise and warning screed,
     That to conceal,
Unto the ordinary man
Is often more alluring than
     To ALL reveal.

RAGETTY DOLL

Rosemary has of dolls a dozen,
    Yet she disdains them all;
While Marie Rose, her pauper cousin
    Has just an old rag doll.
But you should see her mother it,
    And with her kisses smother it.

A twist of twill, a hank of hair,
    Fit for the rubbish bin;
How Rosemary with scorn would stare
    At its pathetic grin!
Yet Marie Rose can lover it,
    And with her kisses cover it.

Rosemary is a pampered pet;
    She sniffs a dainty nose
Of scorn at ragged dolls, and yet
    My love's with Marie Rose,
In garret corner shy and sweet,
    With rag doll Marguerite.

Though kin they are, a gulf will grow
    Between them with the years;
For one a life of love will know,
    The other toil and tears:
Perhaps that shabby rag doll knows
    The rue of Marie Rose.

GIGNOL

Addict of Punch and Judy shows
    I was when I was small;
My kiddy laughter, I suppose,
    Rang louder than them all.
The Judge with banter I would bait,
    The Copper was a wretch;
But oh how I would hiss my hate
    For grim Jack Ketch.

Although a grandsire grey I still
    Love Punch and Judy shows,
And with my toddlers help to fill
    Enthusiastic rows.
How jolly is their mirth to see,
    And what a sigh they fetch,
When Punch begs to be shown and he
    Jerks up Jack Ketch.

Heigh ho! No more I watch the play;
    It is the audience
That gives me my delight today,—
    Such charm of innocence!
Immortal mimes! It seems to me,
    Could I re-live my span,
With gusto I would like to be
    A Punch and Judy Man.

A SNIFTER

After working hard all day
       In the office,
How much worse on homeward way
       My old cough is!
Barney's Bar is gaily lit,
       Let me stop there;
Just to buck me up a bit
       Have a drop there.

As I stand beside the screen
       Hesitating,
I have thought of how Noreen
       Will be waiting;
Baby Patsy in her lap
       Gay and laughing,
While at Barney's foaming tap
       I am quaffing.

Barney's Bar is mighty bright,
       Looks so cheery.
Wonder what I'll drink tonight?
       Gee! I'm weary.
Will I have Scotch or Rye?
       Bourbon maybe . . .
Then I see with mental eye
       Wife and baby.

So I say 'tis malted milk
      I'll be skoffin';
Sooth my throttle sleek as silk,
      Ease my coughin' . . .
Say, I love them two to death,
      Sure they miss me:
With no whisky on my breath
      How they'll kiss me!

SECOND CHILDHOOD

When I go on my morning walk,
    Because I'm mild,
If I be in the mood to talk
    I choose a child.
I'd rather prattle with a lass
    Of tender age
Than converse in the high-brow class
    With college sage.

I love the touch of silken hand
    That softly clings;
In old of age I understand
    Life's little things.
I love the lisp of tiny tongue
    And trusting eyes;
These are the joys that keep me young
    As daylight dies.

For as to second childhood I
    Draw gently near,
With happy heart I see the why
    Children are dear.
So wise Professor, go your way,—
    I am beguiled
To wistful loving by the gay
    Laugh of a child.

TWO CHILDREN

Give me your hand, oh little one!
    Like children be we two;
Yet I am old, my day is done
    That barely breaks for you.
A baby-basket hard you hold,
    With in it cherries four:
You cherish them as men do gold,
    And count them o'er.

And then you stumble in your walk;
    The cherries scattered lie.
You pick them up with foolish talk
    And foolish glad am I,
When you wipe one quite clean of dust
    And give it unto me;
So in the baby-basket just
    Are three.

All this is simple, I confess,
    A moment piled with peace;
Yet loving men have died for less,
    And will till time shall cease. . . .
A silken hand in crinkled one—
    O Little Innocence!
O blessed moment in the sun
    E'er I go hence!

RHYMES FOR REALITY

LOCAL LAD

I never saw a face so bright
    With brilliant blood and joy,
As was the grinning mug last night
    Of Dick, our local boy,
When with a clumsy, lucky clout
    He knocked the champion out.

A week ago he swung a pick
    And sweated in a ditch.
Tonight he's togged up mighty slick,
    And fancies himself rich.
With floozies, fine food, bubbly drink
    He'll go to hell I think.

Unless they make another match;
    And if they do I guess
The champion won't have a scratch,
    But Dick will be a mess;
His map will be a muck of gore
    As he sprawls on the floor.

Then he'll go back his pick to swing,
    And sweat deep in the mud . . .
Yet still I see him in the ring,
    So gay with glee and blood,
Dancing a jig and holding high
    His gloves to climb the sky.

FINNIGAN'S FINISH

They thought I'd be a champion;
  They boasted loud of me.
A dozen victories I'd won,
  The Press was proud of me.
I saw myself with glory crowned,
  And would, beyond a doubt,
Till last night in the second round
  A Dago knocked me out.

It must have been an accident;
  I cannot understand.
For I was so damn confident
  I'd lick him with one hand.
I bounded in the ring to cheers;
  I panted for the fray:
Ten minutes more with hoots and jeers
  They bore me limp away.

I will not have the nerve to face
  The sporting mob today;
The doll I fell for—my disgrace
  Will feel and fade away.
Last night upon the brink of fame
  No favour did I lack:
Tomorrow from the sink of shame
  I'll beg my old job back.

CARDIAC

A mattock high he swung;
I watched him at his toil;
With never gulp of lung
He gashed the ruddy soil.
Thought I, I'd give my wealth
        To have his health.

With fortune I would part,
And privilege resign,
Could I but have his heart,
And he have mine . . .
Then suddenly I knew
        My wish was true.

Like him I swung: with awe
He marked my steady breath.
Then suddenly I saw
That he was sick to death.
My heart in him was frail
        And seemed to fail.

Said I: 'Take back your heart
And I will bear with mine.
Poor lad! All wealth apart
'Tis murder I design.
Not all a Nabob's wealth
        Is worth your health.'

SECRETARY

My Master is a man of might
    With manners like a hog;
He makes me slave from morn to night
    And treats me like a dog.
He thinks there's nothing on this earth
    His money cannot buy,
And claims to get full wages worth
    From hirelings such as I.

But does he? Though a Man of State,
    And fabulously rich,
He little guesses that his mate
    Is just a bonny bitch.
For he is grey and gross and fat,
    While I am tall and slim,
And when he's gone it happens that
    I take the place of him.

Oh God! The beauty of the blow
    When I will blast his life;
When I will laugh and let him know
    My mistress is his wife.
Today a doormat for his feet,
    He loves to see me squirm . . .
Tomorrow,—how revenge is sweet!
    The turning of the worm.

FOUR-FOOT SHELF

'Come, see,' said he, 'my four-foot shelf,
      A forty volume row;
And every one I wrote myself,
      But that, of course, you know.'
I stared, I searched a memory dim,
      For though an author too,
Somehow I'd never heard of him,—
      None of his books I knew.

Said I: 'I'd like to borrow one,
      Fond memories to recall.'
Said he: 'I'll gladly give you *some,*
      And autograph them all.'
And so a dozen books he brought,
      And signed tome after tome:
Of course I thanked him quite a lot,
      And took them home.

So now I have to read his work,
      Though dry as dust it be;
No portion of it may I shirk,
      Lest he should question me.
This tale is true,—although it looks
      To me a bloody shame,
A guy could father forty books,
      Yet no one know his name.

THE ACTOR

Enthusiastic was the crowd
    That hailed him with delight;
The wine was bright, the laughter loud
    And glorious the night.
But when at dawn he drove away
    With echo of their cheer,
To where his little daughter lay,
    Then he knew— Fear.

How strangely still the house! He crept
    On tip-toe to the bed;
And there she lay as if she slept
    With candles at her head.
Her mother died to give her birth,
    An angel child was she;
To him the dearest one on earth . . .
    How could it be?

'O God! If she could only live,'
    He thought with bitter pain,
'How gladly, gladly would I give
    My glory and my gain.
I have created many a part,
    And many a triumph known;
Yet here is one with breaking heart
    I play alone.'

Beside the hush of her his breath
    Came with a sobbing sigh.
He babbled: 'Sweet, you play at death . . .
    'Tis I who die.'

THE HOMICIDE

They say she speeded wanton wild
    When she was warm with wine;
And so she killed a little child,
    (Could have been yours or mine).
The Judge's verdict was not mild,
    And heavy was the fine.

And yet I see her driving still,
    But maybe with more care . . .
Oh I should hate a child to kill
    With vine leaves in my hair:
I think that I should grieve until
    Life was too bleak to bear.

I think that I would see each day
    That child in beauty grow.
How she would haunt me in her play.
    And I would watch her go
To school a-dancing on her way,
    With gladness all aglow!

And then one day I might believe,
    With angel eyes ashine,
She'd say to me: 'Please do not grieve,
    Maybe the fault was mine.
Take heart,—to Heaven's comfort cleave,
    For am I not divine!'

I think I know how I would feel
    If I a child should slay;
The rest of living I would kneel
    And for God's pity pray . . .
Madam, I saw you at the wheel
    Of your new car today.

THE JUDGEMENT

The Judge looked down, his face was grim,
  He scratched his ear;
The gangster's moll looked up at him
  With eyes of fear.
She thought: 'This guy in velvet gown,
  With balding pate,
Who now on me is looking down,
  Can seal my fate.'

The Judge thought: 'Fifteen years or ten
  I might decree.
Just let me say the word and then
  Go home to tea.
But then this poor wretch might not be
  So long alive . . .'
So with surprise he heard that he
  Was saying 'Five.'

The Judge went home. His daughter's child
  Was five that day;
And with sweet gifts around her piled
  She laughed in play.
Then mused the Judge: 'Life oft bestows
  Such evil odds.
May he who human mercy shows
  Not count on God's?'

POOR POET

'A man should write to please himself,'
    He proudly said.
Well, see his poems on the shelf,
    Dusty, unread.

When he came to my shop each day,
    So peaked and cold,
I'd sneak one of his books away
    And say 'twas sold.

And then by chance he looked below,
    And saw a stack
Of his own work,—speechless with woe
    He came not back.

I hate to think he took to drink,
    And passed away;
I have not heard of him a word
    Unto this day.

A man must write to please himself,
    Of all it's true;
But happy they who spurning pelf—
    Please people too.

TIM

My brother Tim has children ten,
 While I have none.
Maybe that's why he's toiling when
 To ease I've won.
But though I would some of his brood
 Give hearth and care,
I know that not a one he would
 Have heart to spare.

'Tis children that have kept him poor;
 He's clad them neat.
They've never wanted, I am sure,
 For bite to eat.
And though their future may be dim,
 They laugh a lot.
Am I tearful for Brother Tim?
 Oh no, I'm not.

I know he goes to work each day
 With flagging feet.
'Tis hard, even with decent pay,
 To make ends meet.
But when my sterile home I see,
 So smugly prim,
Although my banker bows to me,
 I envy Tim.

BRAVE COWARD

Elisabeth imagines I've
    A yellow streak.
She deems I have no dash and drive,
    Jest dogoned weak.
'A man should be a man,' says Liz
    'Trade blow for blow.'
Poor kid! What my position is,
    She jest don't know.

She jest don't know my old man killed,
    Yea, slew and slew.
As steamy blood he sweetly spilled,
    So could I too.
And though no wrath of heart I show
    When I see red,
I fear no S. O. B. but oh
    Myself I dread.

Though fellers reckon me a dope
    And trigger-shy,
'Tain't nice to dangle on a rope,
    And like Pa die.
So as I belly to the bar
    Meek is my breath . . .
No guts! —Don't needle me too far,
    Elizabeth!

FIDELITY

Being a shorty, as you see,
     A bare five footer,
The why my wife is true to me
     Is my six-shooter.
For every time a guy goes by
     Who looks like a lover,
I polish it to catch his eye,
     And spin it over.

He notes its notches as I say:
     'Believe me, Brother,
If Junie ever goes astray,
     They'll be another.'
A husband has to have a gun
     And guts to pull it:
Few fellows think a bit of fun
     Is worth a bullet.

For June would sit on any knee
     If it wore pants,
Yet she is faithful unto me,
     As gossip grants.
And though I know some six-foot guy
     Would better suit her,
Her virtue triumphs, thanks to my
     Six-shooter.

A BACHELOR

'Why keep a cow when I can buy,'
    Said he, 'the milk I need,'
I wanted to spit in his eye
    Of selfishness and greed;
But did not, for the reason he
    Was stronger than I be.

I told him: ' 'Tis our human fate,
    For better or for worse,
That man and maid should love and mate,
    And little children nurse.
Of course, if you are less than man
    You can't do what we can.

'So many loving maids would wed,
    And wondrous mothers be.'
'I'll buy the love I want,' he said,
    'No squally brats for me.'
. . . I hope the devil stoketh well
    For him a special hell.

LOTTERY TICKET

'A ticket for the lottery
I've purchased every week,' said she
     'For years a score
Though desperately poor am I,
Oh how I've scrimped and scraped to buy
     One chance more.

'Each week I think I'll gain the prize,
And end my sorrows and my sighs,
     For I'll be rich;
Then nevermore I'll eat bread dry,
With icy hands to cry and cry
     And stitch and stitch.'

'Tis true she won the premier prize;
It was of formidable size,
     Ten million francs.
I know, because the man who sold
It to her splenically told
     He got no thanks.

The lucky one was never found,
For she was snugly underground,
     And minus breath;
And with that ticket tucked away,
In some old stocking, so they say,
     She starved to death.

228

SAILOR'S SWEETHEART

He sleeps beside me in the bed;
Upon my breast I hold his head;
Oh how I would that we were wed,
   For he sails in the morning.

I wish I had not been so kind;
But love is fain and passion blind,
While out of sight is out of mind,
   And he ships in the morning.

I feel his bairn stir in my womb;
Poor wee one, born to bitter doom;
How dreary dark will be the gloom,
   When he goes in the morning!

A sailor lad has need to court
A loving lass in every port;
To him it's just a bit of sport . . .
   My heart-break's in the morning.

FAILURE

He wrote a play; by day and night
He strove with passion and delight;
Yet knew, long ere the curtain drop,
His drama was a sorry flop.

In Parliament he sought a seat;
Election Day brought dire defeat;
Yet he had wooed with word and pen
Prodigiously his fellow men.

And then he wrote a lighter play
That made him famous in a day.
He won a seat in Parliament,
And starry was the way he went.

Yet as he neared the door of death
They heard him say with broken breath:
'For all I've spoken, planned and penned,
I'm just a wash-out in the end.'

So are we all; our triumphs won
Are mean by what we might have done.
Our victories that men applaud
Are sordid in the sight of God.

MY SON

I must not let my boy Dick down,
    Knight of the air.
With wings of light he won renown
    Then crashed somewhere.
To fly to France from London town
    I do not dare.

Oh he was such a simple lad
    Who loved the sky;
A modern day Sir Galahad,
    No need to die:
Earthbound he might have been so glad,
    Yet chose to fly.

I ask from where his courage stemmed?
    I've never flown;
Air-travel I have oft condemned,—
    Now I'm alone,
Yet somehow hold the bright belief
    God gave his brief.

So now I must live up to him
    Who won on high
A lustre time will never dim;
    Though coward I,
Let me revere till life be done
    My hero son.

AUNT JANE

When Aunt Jane died we hunted round,
And money everywhere we found.
How much I do not care to say,
But no death duties will we pay,
And Aunt Jane will be well content
We bilked the bloody Government.

While others spent she loved to save,
But couldn't take it to her grave.
While others save we love to spend;
She hated us but in the end
Because she left no Testament
To us all her possessions went.

That is to say they did not find
A lawyer's Will of any kind.
Yet there was one in her own hand,
A Home for Ailing Cats she planned.
Well, you can understand my ire:
Promptly I put it in the fire.

In misery she chose to die,
Yet we will make her money fly.
And as we mourn for poor Aunt Jane
The thought alleviates our pain:
Perhaps her savings in the end
Gave her more joy than we who spend.

THE ARTIST

All day with brow of anxious thought
    The dictionary through,
Amid a million words he sought
    The sole one that would do.
He wandered on from pub to pub
    Yet never ceased to seek
With burning brain and pencil stub
    The Word Unique.

Said he: 'I'll nail it down or die.
    Oh Heaven help me, pray!'
And then a heavy car dashed by,
    And he was in the way.
They rushed him to the hospital,
    And though his chance was bleak,
He cried: 'I'll croak, but find I shall
    The Word Unique.'

They reckoned he was off his head,
    And could be it was so;
For as they bent above his bed
    He mumbled soft and low.
And then a name they heard him speak,
    Yet did not deem it odd . . .
At last he'd found the Word Unique,—
    Just God.

BELATED CONSCIENCE

To buy for school a copy-book
    I asked my Dad for two-pence;
He gave it with a gentle look,
    Although he had but few pence.
'Twas then I proved myself a crook
    And came a moral cropper,
I bought a penny copy-book
    And blued the other copper.

I spent it on a sausage roll
    Gulped down with guilt suggestion,
To the damnation of my soul
    And awful indigestion.
Poor Dad! His job was hard to hold;
    His mouths to feed were many;
Were he alive a millionfold
    I'd pay him for his penny.

Now nigh the grave I think with grief,
    Though other sins are many,
I am a liar and a thief
    'Cause once I stole a penny:
Yet be he pious as a friar
    It is my firm believing,
That every man has been a liar
    And most of us done thieving.

OLD ENGINE DRIVER

For five and twenty years I've run
  A famous train;
But now my spell of speed is done,
  No more I'll strain
My sight along the treadless tracks,
  The gleamy rails:
My hand upon the throttle slacks,
  My vision fails.

No more I'll urge my steed of steel
  Through hostile night;
No more the mastery I'll feel
  Of monster might.
I'll miss the hiss of giant steam,
  The clank, the roar;
The agony of brakes that scream
  I'll hear no more.

Oh I have held within my hand
  A million lives;
And now my son takes command
  And proudly drives;
While from my cottage wistfully
  I watch his train,
And wave and wave and seem to see
  Myself again.

TO A TYCOON

Since much has been your mirth
   And fair your fate,
Friend, leave your lot of earth
   Less desolate.
With frailing overdue,
   Why don't you try
The bit of God in you
   To justify?

Try to discern the grace
   All greed above,
That may uplift the race
   To realm of love.
For in you is a spark,
   A heaven-glow,
That will illume the dark
   Before you go.

Aye, though it be that you
   To Faith are blind,
There's one thing you can do,
   It's—just be kind.
The anguish understand,
   Of hearts that bleed:
Friend, lend a helping hand
   To those in need.

COMRADES

Three Holies sat in sacred place
    And quaffed celestial wine,
As they discussed the human race
    With dignity divine.
Said they: 'Although in doctrine we
    May differ more or less,
In spirit stoutly we agree
    Religion's a success.'

Said One: 'I praise the pride of war,
    The Faith that mocks at fear;
Desire of death in battle for
    It bringeth Heaven near.'
The Second said: ' 'Tis Peace I preach,
    And hate of human strife;
The sufferance of pain I teach,
    The sanctity of life.'

Then said the Third: 'Love I proclaim
    The goal of human good . . .
Yet are we not all three the same
    In holy brotherhood?'
And so they went forth hand in hand,
    Wending a starry way,—
Mohamet, gentle Buddha and
    He of Gethsemenè.

SACRIFICE

I gave an eye to save from night
  A babe born blind;
And now with eager semi-sight
  Vast joy I find
To think a child can share with me
  Earth ecstasy!

Delight of dawn with dewy gleam
  On damask rose;
Crimson and gold as pennons stream
  Where sunset flows;
And sight most nigh to paradise,
  Star-studded skies.

Ah! How in old of age I feel,
  E'er end my days,
Could I star-splendoured sky reveal
  To childish gaze,
Not one eye would I give, but two,—
  Well, wouldn't you?

LYRICS FOR LEVITY

FAREWELL TO VERSE

In youth when oft my muse was dumb,
      My fancy nighly dead,
To make my inspiration come
      I stood upon my head;
And thus I let the blood down flow
      Into my cerebellum,
And published every Spring or so
      Slim tomes in vellum.

Alas! I am rheumatic now,
      Grey is my crown;
I can no more with brooding brow
      Stand upside-down.
I fear I might in such a pose
      Burst brain blood-vessel;
And that would be a woeful close
      To my rhyme wrestle.

If to write verse I must reverse
      I fear I'm stymied;
In ink of prose I must immerse
      A pen de-rhymèd.
No more to spank the lyric lyre
      Like Keats or Browning,
May I inspire the Sacred Fire
      By Upside-downing.

TRIUMPH

Why am I full of joy although
 It drizzles on the links?
Why am I buying *Veuve Cliquot,*
 And setting up the drinks?
Why stand I like a prince amid
 My pals and envy none?
Ye gods of golf! Today I did
 A Hole in One.

I drove my ball to heaven high,
 It over-topped the hill;
I tried to guess how it would lie,
 If on the fairway still.
I climbed the rise, so sure I'd hit
 It straight towards the green:
I looked and looked,—no trace of it
 Was to be seen.

My partner putted to the pin,
 Then hoarse I heard him call;
And lo! So snug the hole within
 Gleamed up my ball.
Yea, it was mine. Oh what a thrill!
 What dandy drive I'd done
By luck,—well, grant a little skill,
 I'd holed in one.

Say that my score is eighty odd,
　　And though I won't give up,—
Say that as round the course I plod,
　　I never win a cup.
Say that my handicap's nineteen,
　　And of my game make fun,
But holler: 'On the seventh green
　　HE HOLED IN ONE.'

PIPE SMOKER

Because I love the soothing weed
      And am of sober type,
I'd choose me for a friend in need
      A man who smokes a pipe.
A cove who hasn't much to say,
      And spits into the fire,
Puffing like me a pipe of clay,
      Corn-cob or briar.

A chap original of thought,
      With cheery point of view,
Who has of gumption quite a lot,
      And streaks of humour too.
He need not be a whiskered sage,
      With wisdom over-ripe:
Just give me in the old of age
      A pal who smokes a pipe.

A cigarette may make for wit,
      Although I like it not;
A good cigar, I must admit,
      Gives dignity to thought.
But as my glass of grog I sip
      I never, never gripe
If I have for companionship
      A guy who smokes a pipe.

RELAX

Do you recall that happy hike
        With bundles on our backs?
How near to heaven it was like
        To blissfully relax!
In cosy tavern of good cheer
        To doff our heavy packs,
And with a mug of foamy beer
        Relax.

Learn to relax: to clean the mind
        Of fear and doubt and care,
And in vacuity to find
        The perfect peace that's there.
With lassitude of heart and hand,
        When every sinew slacks,
How good to rest the old bean and
        Relax, relax.

Just sink back in an easy chair
        For forty winks or so,
And fold your hands as if in prayer,
        —That helps a lot, you know.
Forget that you are you awhile,
        And pliable as wax,
Just beatifically smile . . .
        Relax, relax, relax.

SUCCESSFUL FAILURE

I wonder if successful men
      Are always happy?
And do they sing with gusto when
      Springtime is sappy?
Although I am of snow-white hair
      And nighly mortal,
Each time I sniff the April air
      I chortle.

I wonder if a millionaire
      Jigs with enjoyment,
Having such heaps of time to spare
      For daft employment.
For as I dance the Highland Fling
      My glee is muckle,
And doping out new songs to sing
      I chuckle.

I wonder why so soon forgot
      Are fame and riches;
Let cottage comfort be my lot
      With well-worn britches.
As in a pub a poor unknown,
      Brown ale quaffing,
To think of all I'll never own,—
      I'm laughing.

THE RECEPTIONIST

France is the fairest land on earth,
      Lovely to heart's desire,
And twice a year I span its girth,
      Its beauty to admire.
But when a pub I seek each night,
      To my profound vexation
On form they hand me I've to write
      My occupation.

So once in a derisive mood
      My pen I nibbled;
And though I know I never should:
      'Gangster' I scribbled.
But as the clerk with startled face
      Looked stark suspicion,
I blurred it out and in its place
      Put 'Politician.'

Then suddenly dissolved his frown;
      His face fused to a grin,
As humorously he set down
      The form I handed in.
His shrug was eloquent to view.
      Quoth he: 'What's in a name?
In France, alas! the lousy two
      Are just the same.'

PROFANE POET

Oh how it would enable me
    To titillate my vanity
If you should choose to label me
    A Poet of Profanity!
For I've been known with vulgar slang
    To stoke the Sacred Fire,
And even used a word like 'hang',
    Suggesting ire.

Yea, I've been slyly told, although
    It savours of inanity,
In print the ladies often show
    A failing for profanity.
So to delight the dears I try,
    And often in the past
In fabricating sonnets I
    Have fulminated: 'Blast!'

I know I shock the sober folk
    Who doubt my lyric sanity,
And readers of my rhyme provoke
    By publishing profanity,
But oh a hale and hearty curse
    Is very dear to me,
And so I end this bit of verse
    With d— and d— and d—!

FAMILIARITY

Familiarity some claim
      Can breed contempt,
So from it let it be your aim
      To be exempt.
Let no one exercise his brawn
      To slap your back,
Lest he forget your name is John,
      And call you Jack.

To those who crash your private pew
      Be sour as krout;
Don't let them see the real 'you,'
      And bawl you out.
Don't call your Cousin William—Bill,
      But formal be.
Have care! Beware and shun famil—
      Iarity.

I'm quite polite. My hat I doff
      But little say.
I give the crowd the big brush-off,
      And go my way.
To common folk I do not freeze,
      I am no snob:
But though my name is Robert, please
      Don't call me BOB.

OBESITY

With belly like a poisoned pup
    Said I: 'I must give bacon up;
And also, I profanely fear,
    I must abandon bread and beer
That make for portliness they say;
    Yet of them copiously today
I ate with an increasingly sense
        Of grievous corpulence.

I like a lot of things I like.
    Too bad that I must go on strike
Against pork sausages and mash,
    Spaghetti and fried corn-beef hash.
I deem he is a lucky soul
    Who has no need of girth control;
For in the old of age: *'Il faut*
        Souffrir pour etre beau.'

Yet let me not be unconsoled:
    So many greybeards I behold,
Distinguished in affairs of State,
    In culture counted with the Great,
Have tummies with a shameless bulge,
    And so I think I'll still indulge
In eats I like without a qualm,
        And damn my diaphragm!

TRIPE

When I was young and moron
        I doted on Hall Caine;
Corelli I would pore on,
        Despite high-brow disdain.
Aye, though them critic fellers
        Damned both in bitter type,
Insisting them best-sellers
        Were just Tripe.

Today I'm reading Cronin,
        Du Maurier and such,
And critics still are groanin'
        And griping overmuch.
But I, their scorn unheeding,
        Forget to light my pipe,
So rapt am I a-reading
        Of their Tripe.

For though my head is hoary,
        Still moron is my heart;
I love a darned good story
        With action from the start.
Aye, though the critics suffer
        And artistically gripe,
Just write me down a duffer
        Loving Tripe.

TOURIST

'Twas in a village in Lorraine
    Whose name I quite forget,
I found I needfully was fain
    To buy a *serviette*.
I sought a shop wherein they sell
    Such articles as these,
And told a smiling mademoiselle;
    'I want a towel, please.'

'Of kinds,' said she, 'I've only two,'
    And took the bundles down;
And one was coloured azure blue,
    And one was khaki brown.
With doubt I scratched my hoary head;
    The quality was right;
The size too, yet I gravely said:
    'Too bad you haven't white.'

That pretty maid had sunny hair,
    Her gaze was free from guile,
And while I hesitated there
    She watched me with a smile.
Then as I went to take the blue
    She said 'Non' meaning no.
'Ze khaki ones are best, M'sieu:
    Ze *dirts* zey do not show.'

THE BUYERS

Father drank himself to death,—
  Quite enjoyed it.
Urged to draw a sober breath
  He'd avoid it.
'Save your sympathy,' said Dad;
  'Never sought it.
Hob-nail liver, gay and glad,
  Sure,—I bought it.'

Uncle made a heap of dough,
  Ponies playing.
'Easy come and easy go,'
  Was his saying.
Though he died in poverty
  Fit he thought it,
Grinning with philosophy:
  'Guess I bought it.'

Auntie took the way of sin,
  Seeking pleasure;
Lovers came, her heart to win,
  Bearing treasure.
Sickness smote,—with lips that bled
  Brave she fought it;
Smiling on her dying bed:
  'Dears, I bought it.'

My decades of life are run,
                Eight precisely;
Yet I've lost a lot of fun
                Living wisely.
Too much piety don't pay,
                Time has taught it;
Hadn't guts to go astray;
Life's a bloody bore today,—
                Well, I've bought it.

PROCREATION

It hurts my pride that I should be
  The issue of a night of lust;
Yet even Bishops, you'll agree,
  Obey the biologic 'must';
Though no doubt with more dignity
  Than we of layman dust.

I think the Lord made a mistake
  When he designed the human race,
That man and angel in the make
  Should have brutality for base.
Jehovah might have planned at least
  Not to confound us with the beast.

So with humiliation I
  Think of my basic origin;
And yet with some relief I sigh,—
  I might have been conceived in sin;
Instead of being, I believe,
  The offspring of a nuptial eve.

So when I look in beauty's face,
    Or that of king or saint or sage,
It seems to me I darkly trace
    Their being to a rutting rage . . .
Had I been Deity's adviser
    Meseems I might have planned it wiser.

SPATS

When young I was a Socialist
    Despite my tender years;
No blessed chance I ever missed
    To slam the profiteers.
Yet though a fanatic I was,
    And cursed aristocrats,
The Party chucked me out because
    I sported Spats.

Aye, though on soap boxes I stood,
    And spouted in the parks,
They grizzled that my foot-wear would
    Be disavowed by Marx.
It's buttons of a pearly sheen
    Bourgois they deemed and thus
They told me; 'You must choose between
    Your spats and us.'

Alas! I loved my gaitered feet
    Of smoothly fitting fawn;
They were so snappy and so neat,
    A gift from Uncle John
Who had a fortune in the Bank
    That one day might be mine:
'Give up my spats!' said I, 'I thank
    You—but resign.'

Today when red or pink I see
      In stripy pants of state,
I think of how they lost in me
      A demon of debate.
I muse as Leaders strut about
      In frock-coats and high hats . . .
The bloody party chucked me out
      Because of Spats.

THE SHORTER CATECHISM

I burned my fingers on the stove
      And wept with bitterness;
But poor old Auntie Maggie strove
      To comfort my distress.
Said she: 'Think, lassie, how you'll **burn**
      Like any wicked besom
In fires of hell if you don't learn
      Your Shorter Catechism.'

A man's chief end is it began,
      (No mention of a woman's),
To glorify—I think it ran,
      The God who made poor humans.
And as I learned, I thought: if this—
      (My distaste growing stronger),
The Shorter Catechism is,
      Lord save us from the longer.

The years have passed and I begin
      (Although I'm far from clever),
To doubt if when we die in sin
      Our bodies grill forever.
Now I've more surface space to burn,
      Since I am tall and lissom,
I think it's hell enough to learn
      The Shorter Catechism.

THE BATTLE

Dames should be doomed to dungeons
Who masticate raw onions.

She was the cuddly kind of Miss
      A man can love to death;
But when I sought to steal a kiss
      I wilted from a breath
With onion odour so intense
      I lost my loving sense.

Yet she was ever in my thought
      Like some exotic flower,
And so a garlic bulb I bought
      And chewed it by the hour;
Then when we met I thrilled to see
      'Twas she who shrank from me.

So breath to breath we battled there,
      To dominate each other;
And though her onions odious were,
      My garlic was a smother;
Till loth I said: 'If we would kiss
      Let's call an armistice.

'Now we have proved that we are true
      To our opinions,
My garlic I'll give up if you
      Give up your onions.'
And so next day with honey sips
      How sweet her lips!

ERICO

Oh darling Eric, why did you
For my fond affection sue,
And then with surgeons artful aid
Transform yourself into a maid?
So now in petticoats you go
And people call you Erico.

Sometimes I wonder if they can
Change me in turn into a man;
Then after all we might get wed
And frolic on a feather bed:
Although I do not see how we
Could ever have a family.

Oh dear! Oh dear! It's so complex.
Why must they meddle with our sex.
My Eric was a handsome 'he,'
But now he—oh excuse me—she
Informs me that I must forget
I was his blond Elizabet.

Alas! These scientists of Sweden
I curse, who've robbed me of my Eden;
Who with their weird hormones inhuman
Can make a man into a woman.
Alas, poor Eric! . . . Erico
I wish you were in Jerico.

THE CENTENARIANS

I asked of ancient gaffers three
*   The way of their ripe living,*
And this is what they told to me
*   Without misgiving.*

The First: 'The why I've lived so long,
        To my fond recollection
Is that for women, wine and song
        I've had a predilection.
Full many a bawdy stave I've sung
        With wenches of my choosing,
But of the joys that kept me young
        The best was boozing.'

The Second: 'I'm a sage revered
        Because I was a fool,
And with the bourgeon of my beard
        I kept my ardour cool.
On health I have conserved my hold
        By never dissipating:
And that is why a hundred old
        I'm celebrating.'

The Third: 'The explanation I
     Have been so long a-olding,
Is that to wash I never try,
     Despite conjugal scolding.
I hate the sight of soap and so
     I seldom change my shirt:
Believe me, Brother, there is no
     Preservative like dirt.'

So there you have the reasons three
     Why age may you rejoice:
Booze, squalour and temerity,—
     Well, you may take your choice.
Yet let me say, although it may
     Your egoism hurt,
Of all the three it seems to me
     The best is DIRT.

SURTAX

When I was young and Scottish I
   Allergic was to spending;
I put a heap of bawbees by,
   But now my life is ending,
Although I would my hoarded pelf
   Impetuously scatter,
Each day I live I find myself
   Financially fatter.

Though all the market I might buy,
   There's nothing to my needing;
I only have one bed to lie,
   One mouth for feeding.
So what's the good of all that dough
   Accumulating daily?
I should have spent it long ago
   In living gaily.

So take my tip, my prudent friend,
   Without misgiving;
Don't guard your fortune to the end,
   But blow it living.
Better on bubbly be it spent,
   And chorus cuties,
Than pay it to the Government
   For damned Death Duties.

PLEBEIAN PLUTOCRAT

I own a gorgeous Cadillac,
    A chauffeur garbed in blue;
And as I sit behind his back
    His beefy neck I view.
Yet let me whisper, though you may
    Think me a queer old cuss,
From Claude I often sneak away
    To board a bus.

A democrat, I love the crowd,
    The bustle and the din;
The market wives who gab aloud
    As they go out and in.
I chuckle as I pay my dime,
    With mien meticulous:
You can't believe how happy I'm;
    Aboard a bus.

The driver of my Cadillac
    Has such a haughty sneer;
I'm sure he would give me the sack
    If he beheld me here.
His horror all my friends would share
    Could they but see me thus:
A gleeful multi-millionaire
    Aboard a bus.

JANE

My daughter Jane makes dresses
For beautiful Princesses;
But though she's plain is Jane,
Of needlework she's vain,
And makes such pretty things
For relatives of Kings.

She reads the picture papers
Where Royalties cut capers,
And often says to me:
'How wealthy they must be,
That nearly every day
A new robe they can pay.'

Says I: 'If your Princesses
Could *fabric* pretty dresses,
Though from a throne they stem
I would think more of them.
Peeress and shopgirl are
To my mind on a par.'

Says Jane: 'But for their backing
I might be sewing sacking.
Instead, I work with joy
In exquisite employ,
Embroidering rich dresses
For elegant Princesses . . .
Damn social upsetters
Who criticise their betters!'

WASHERWIFE

The aged Queen who passed away
Had sixty servants, so they say;
Twice sixty hands her shoes to tie:
Two soapy ones have I.

The old Queen had of beds a score;
A cot have I and ask no more.
For when the last is said and done
One can but die in one.

The old Queen rightly thought that she
Was better than the likes o' me;
And yet I'm glad despite her grace
I am not in her place.

The old Queen's gone and I am here,
To eat my tripe and drink my beer,
Athinkin' as I wash my clothes:
We must have monarchs, I suppose . . .
Well, well,—'Taint no skin off my nose!

LAND MINE

A grey gull hovered overhead,
    Then wisely flew away.
'In half a jiffy you'll be dead,'
    I thought I heard it say;
As there upon the railway line,
    Checking an urge to cough,
I laboured to de-fuse the mine
    That had not yet gone off.

I tapped around the time-clock rim,
    Then something worried me.
I heard the singing of a hymn:
    Nearer my God to Thee.
That damned Salvation Army band!
    I phoned back to the boys:
'Please tell them,—they will understand,—
    Cut out the bloody noise!'

Silence . . . I went to work anew,
    And then I heard a tick
That told me the blast was due,—
    I never ran so quick.
I heard the fury-roar behind;
    The earth erupted hell,
As hoisted high and stunned and blind
    Into a ditch I fell.

Then when at last I crawled from cover,
    My hands were bloody raw;
And I was blue and bruised all over,
    And this is what I saw:
All pale, but panting with elation,
    And very much unstuck,
There was the Army of Salvation
    Emerging from the muck.

And then I heard the Captain saying:
    ' 'Twas Heaven heard our pleas;
For there anight we all were praying
    Down on our bended knees.
'Twas little hope your comrades gave you,
    Though we had faith divine . . .
The blessed Lord stooped down to save you,
    But Gosh! *He cut it fine.*'

THE BIOLOGIC URGE

Confound all aberrations which
        Make men do foolish things,
Like buying bracelets for a bitch,
        Or witless wedding rings.
As if we had not woe enough
        Our simple souls to vex,
Without that brand of trouble stuff
        We label Sex.

Has science not the means produced
        For human propagation,
By artificially induced
        Insemination?
Then every man might be a priest,
        And every maid a nun . . .
Oh well, as chaste as they at least,—
        But nix on fun.

Just think how we would grow in grace
        If lust we could exclude;
Then innocence might take its place,
        —Well, in a sense it could.
How we would be forever free
        From passions that perplex!
What peace on earth if only we
        Could outlaw Sex!

TREAT 'EM ROUGH

First time I dared propose,
        A callow lad was I;
I donned my Sunday clothes,
        I wore my Old School Tie.
Awaiting me Louise
        Was dolled to beat the band,
So going on my knees
        I begged her hand.

Oh yes, she gave me her hand,—
        A box upon the ear;
I could not understand,
        I blinked away a tear.
Then scornfully she said:
        'Next time you kneel before
A maid, young man don't spread
        Your hankey on the floor.'

So next time I proposed,
        Thinks I, I'll treat 'em rough.
Her name was Lily Rose,
        I gave her he-man stuff.
I yanked her on my knee,
        And as her ear I bit,
To my amazement she
        Seemed to like it.

The old cave-men knew best;
      Grab girlies by the hair,
And though they may protest
      Drag them into your lair.
So young men seeking mates,
      Take my tip, if rejected:
A modern maid just hates
      To be respected.

COWS

I love to watch my seven cows
In meads of buttercups abrowse,
       With guilded knees;
But even more I love to see
Them chew the cud so tranquilly
       In twilight ease.

Each is the image of content
From fragrant hours in clover spent,
       'Mid leaf and bud;
As up and down without a pause
Mechanically move their jaws
       To chew the cud.

Friend, there's a hope for me and you:
Let us resolve to chew and chew
       With molars strong;
The man who learns to masticate
With patience may control his fate,
       His life prolong.

In salivation is salvation:
So if some silly little nation
      Should bathe in blood,
Let's take a lesson from the cow,
And learn in life's long gloaming how
      To chew the cud.

DARK GLASSES

Sweet maiden, why disguise
The beauty of your eyes
       With glasses black?
Although I'm well aware
That you are more than fair,
       Allure you lack.
For as I stare at you
I ask if brown or blue
       Your optics are?
But though I cannot see,
I'm sure that each must be
       Bright as a star.

They may be green or grey,
'Tis very hard to say,
       Or violet;
The lovelight in their glow
Alas, I'll never know,
       To my regret.
In some rhyme-book I've read,
A lady bard has said,
       And deemed it true,
Men will not bite the necks
Of sweeties who wear specs,—
       Young man, would you?

But though they balk romance,
Columbus took a chance,
     And so would I;
Even with orbs unseen
I'd fain make you my queen
     And you en-sky.
Alas I see you go,
And I will never know
     Your pupils tint;
So o'er a lonely drink
I force myself to think:
     Damsel, you squint!

POET AND PEER

They asked the Bard of Ayr to dine;
The banquet hall was fit and fine,
    With gracing it a Lord;
The poet came; his face was grim
To find the place reserved for him
    Was at the butler's board.

So when the gentry called him in,
He entered with a knavish grin
    And sipped a glass of wine;
But when they asked would he recite
Something of late he'd chanced to write
    He ettled to decline.

Then with a sly, sardonic look
He opened up a little book
    Containing many a gem;
And as they sat in raiment fine,
So smug and soused with rosy wine,
    This verse he read to them.

'You see yon birkie caw'ed a Lord,
    Who struts and stares an' a' that,
Though hundreds worship at his word
    He's but a coof for a' that.
For a' that and a' that,
    A man's a man for a' that.

He pointed at that portly Grace
Who glared with apoplectic face,
     While others stared with gloom;
Then having paid them all he owed,
Burns, Bard of Homespun, smiled and strode
     Superbly from the room.

TOILET SEATS

While I am emulating Keats
My brother fabrics toilet seats,
The which, they say, are works of art,
Aesthetic features of the mart;
So exquisitely are they made
With plastic of a pastel shade,
Of topaz, ivory or rose,
Inviting to serene repose.

Rajahs I'm told have seats of gold,—
(They must, I fear, be very cold).
But Tom's have thermostatic heat,
With sympathy your grace to greet.
Like silver they are neon lit,
Making a halo as you sit:
Then lo! they play with dulset tone
A melody by Mendelssohn.

Oh were I lyrical as Yeats
I would not sing of toilet seats,
But rather serenade a star,—
Yet I must take things as they are.
For even kings must coyly own
Them as essential as a throne:
So as I tug the Muse's teats
I envy Tom his toilet seats.

DISTRACTED DRUGGIST

'A shilling's worth of quinine, please,'
    The customer demanded.
The druggist went down on his knees
    And from a cupboard handed
The waiting man a tiny flask:
    'Here, Sir, is what you ask.'

The buyer paid and went away,
    The druggist rubbed his glasses,
Then sudden shouted in dismay:
    'Of all the silly asses!'
And out into the street he ran
    To catch the speeding man.

Cried he: 'That quinine that you bought,
    (Since all may errors make),
I find was definitely not,—
    I sold you strychnine by mistake.
Two shillings is its price, and so
    Another bob you owe.'

NAVELS

Men have navels more or less;
       Some are neat, some not.
Being fat I must confess
       Mine is far from hot.
Woman's is a pearly ring,
       Lovely to my mind;
So of it to shyly sing
       I am inclined.

I believe in nudity.
       Female forms divine
Should be bared for all to see
       In colour and in line.
So dear ladies, recognise
       The dimpling of your waist
Has approval in my eyes,
       Favour in my taste.

Darlings, please you, paint them gold,
       Or some pastel hue;
Make them starry to behold,
       Witching to the view.
Though I know I never should
       Say such things as this:
How a rosebud navel would
       Be sweet to kiss!

MY CONSOLATION

'Nay; I don't need a hearing aid'
    I told Mama-in-law;
'For if I had I'd be afraid
    Of your eternal jaw;
Although at me you often shout,
    I'm undisturbed;
To tell the truth I can't make out
    A single word.'

And it's the same with others who
    Attempt to gab at me;
I listen to their point of view
    And solemnly agree.
To story stale and silly joke
    Stone deaf's my ear;
Each day a dozen stupid folk
    I fail to hear.

So silence that should be my grief
    Is my escape and shield;
From spiteful speech and base relief
    My aural sense is sealed.
And in my cosy cot of peace
    I close the door,
Praising the gods for rich relief
    From fool and bore.

WILLIE

'Why did the lady in the lift
  Slap that poor parson's face?'
Said Mother, thinking as she sniffed,
  Of clerical disgrace.

Said Sonny Boy: 'Alas, I know.
  My conscience doth accuse me;
The lady stood upon my toe,
  Yet did not say—"Excuse me!"

'She hurt—and in that crowd confined
  I scarcely could endure it;
So when I pinched her fat behind
  She thought—it was the *Curate.*'

BOXER'S WIFE

She phoned them when the Round was Eight:
    'How is my Joe?' they heard her say.
They answered: 'Gee! He's going great,
        Your guy's Okay.'

She phoned them when the Round was Nine:
    'How is my hero in the fray?'
They yelled: 'He leads; he's doing fine,—
        Joe's sure Okay.'

She phoned them when the Round was Ten:
    'Is it still Okay with my Joe?'
Reluctant came the answer then,—
        No Ma'am, KAYO.

WHAT KISSES HAD JOHN KEATS?

I scanned two lines with some surmise
As over Keats I chanced to pore:
'And there I shut her wild, wild eyes
      With kisses four.'

Says I: 'Why was it only four,
Not five or six or seven?
I think I would have made it more,—
      Even eleven.

'Gee! If she'd lured a guy like me
Into her gelid grot
I'd make that Belle Dame sans Merci
      Sure kiss a lot.

'Them poets have their little tricks;
I think John counted kisses four,
Not two or three or five or six
      To rhyme with "sore." '

THE CENTENARIAN

Great Grandfather was ninety-nine
    And so it was our one dread,
That though his health was superfine
    He'd fail to make the hundred.
Though he was not a rolling stone
    No moss he seemed to gather:
A patriarch of brawn and bone
        Was Great Grandfather.

He should have been senile and frail
    Instead of hale and hearty;
But no, he loved his mug of ale,
    A boisterous old party.
'As frisky as a colt,' said he,
    'A man's allotted span
I've lived but now I plan to be
    A Centenarian.'

Then one night when I called on him
    Oh what a change I saw!
His head was bowed, his eye was dim,
    Down-fallen was his jaw.
Said he: 'Leave me to die, I pray;
    I'm no more bloody use . . .
For in my mouth I found today—
    A tooth that's loose.'

MY TAILS

I haven't worn my evening dress
    For nearly twenty years;
Oh I'm unsocial, I confess,
    A hermit, it appears.
So much moth-balled it's put away,
    And though wee wifie wails,
Never unto my dimmest day
    I'll don my tails.

How slim and trim I looked in them,
    Though I was sixty old;
And now their sleekness I condemn
    To lie in rigid fold.
I have a portrait of myself
    Proud-printed in the Press,
In garb now doomed to wardrobe shelf,—
    My evening dress.

So let this be my last request,
    That when I come to die,
In tails I may be deftly drest,
    With white waistcoat and tie.
No, not for me a vulgar shroud
    My carcass to caress;—
Oh let me do my coffin proud
    In evening dress!

THE PRETTY LADY

He asked the lady in the train
If he might smoke: she smiled consent.
So lighting his cigar and fain
To talk he puffed away content,
Reflecting: how delightful are
        Fair dame and fine cigar.

Then from his bulging wallet he
A photograph with pride displayed,
His charming wife and children three,
When suddenly he was dismayed
To hear her say: 'These notes you've got,—
        I want the lot.'

He scarcely could believe his ears.
He laughed: 'The money isn't mine.
To pay it back would take me years,
And so politely I decline.
Madame, I think you speak in fun:
        Have you a gun?'

She smiled. 'No weapon have I got,
Only my virtue, but I swear
If you don't hand me out the lot
I'll rip my blouse, let down my hair,
Denounce you as a fiend accurst . . ."
        He told her: 'Do your worst.'

She did. Her silken gown she tore,
Let down her locks and pulled the cord
That stopped the train, and from the floor
She greeted engineer and guard:
'I fought and fought in vain,' she cried.
   'Save me,—I'm terrified!'

The man was calm; he stood aloof.
Said he: 'Her game you understand;
But if you doubt, behold the proof
Of innocence is in my hand.'
And as they stared into the car
They saw his logic in a flash . . .
Aloft he held *a lit cigar*
   With two inches of ash.

DERISIVE DITTIES

GYPSY JILL

They're hanging Bill at eight o'clock,
    And millions will applaud.
He killed, and so they have to kill,
    Such is the will of God.
His brother Tom is on my bed
    To keep me comforted.

I see his bleary, blotchy face,
    I hear his sodden snore.
He plans that he can take Bill's place;
    I felt worse than a whore
As in his arms I cried all night,
    Thinking of poor Bill's plight.

I keep my eyes upon the clock;
    It nears the stroke of eight.
I think how bravely Bill will walk
    To meet his gallows fate . . .
His loaded gun is in the tent,—
    I know now what he meant.

Though Tom is boastful he will wed
      With me, no more to part,
I'll put a bullet through his head,
      Another through my heart:
At eight, stone-dead we three will be,
      —Bill, Tom and me.

MY FEUD

I hate my neighbour Widow Green;
    I'd like to claw her face;
But if I did she'd make a scene
    And run me round the place:
For widows are in way of spleen
    A most pugnacious race.

And yet I must do something quick
    To keep the hag in line,
Since her red rooster chose to pick
    Five lettuce heads of mine:
And so I fed it arsenic
    Which it did not decline.

It disappeared, but on my mat
    Before a week had sped
I found Mi-mi, my tabby cat
    And it was stoney dead;
I diagnosed with weeping that
    On strychnine it had fed.

And so I bought a hamburg steak,
    Primed it with powdered glass,
And left it for her dog to take
    With gulping from the grass:
Since then, although I lie awake
    I have not seen it pass.

Well, that's the scoring up to date:
    And as I read a text
From Job to justify my hate
    I wonder who'll be next?
Somehow I feel that one must die,
    Ma Green or I.

MARY ELLEN

It's mighty quiet in the house
    Since Mary Ellen quit me cold;
I've swept the hearth and fed the mouse
    That's getting fat and overbold.
I've bought a pig's foot for the pot
    And soon I'll set the fire alight;
Then I may eat or I may not,
    Depends upon my appetite.

Since Mary Ellen left me lone
    I haven't earned a bloody bob.
I sit and sigh, and mope and moan,
    And bellyache I quit my job.
My money's mostly gone,—I think
    I ought to save it up for food . . .
But no, I'll blow it in for drink,
    Then do a bunk for good.

I watch my mouse his whiskers preen;
    He watches me with wicked glee.
Today—oh God! It's years sixteen
    Since Mary Ellen wed with me.
Oh how the dear girl hated vermin!
    She left rat poison on the shelf . . .
Friend Mouse, your doom I now determine
    Then—how about myself?

HENRY

Mary and I were twenty-two
    When we were wed;
A well-matched pair, right smart to view
    The town's folk said.
For twenty years I have been true
    To nuptial bed.

But oh alas! The march of time,
    Life's wear and tear!
Now I am in my lusty prime
    With pep to spare,
While she looks ten more years than I'm,
    With greying hair.

'Twas on our trip dear friends among,
    To New Orleans,
A stranger's silly trip of tongue
    Kiboshed my dreams:
I heard her say: 'How very young
    His *mother* seems.'

Child-bearing gets a woman down,
    And six had she;
Yet now somehow I feel a clown
    When she's with me;
When cuties smile one cannot frown,
    You must agree.

How often I have heard it said:
     'For happy fate,
In age a girl ten years ahead
     Should choose her mate.'
Now twenty years to Mary wed
     I know too late.

BANK ROBBER

I much admire, I must admit,
  The man who robs a Bank;
It takes a lot of guts and grit,
  For lack of which I thank
The gods: a chap 'twould make of me
  You wouldn't ask to tea.

I do not mean a burglar cove
  Who climbs into a house,
From room to room flash-lit to rove
  As quiet as a mouse;
Ah no, in Crime he cannot rank
  With him who robs a Bank.

Who seemeth not to care a whoop
  For danger at its height;
Who handles what is known as 'soup,'
  And dandles dynamite:
Unto a bloke who can do that
  I doff my bowler hat.

I think he is the kind of stuff
    To be a mighty man
In battlefield,—aye, brave enough
    The Cross Victorian
To win and rise to high command,
    A hero in the land.

What General with all his swank
Has guts enough to rob a Bank!

THE BANDIT

Upon his way to rob a Bank
      He paused to watch a fire;
Though crowds were pressing rank on rank
      He pushed a passage nigher;
Then sudden heard, piercing and wild,
      The screaming of a child.

A Public Enemy was he,
      A hater of the law;
He looked around for bravery
      But only fear he saw;
Then to the craven crowds amaze
      He plunged into the blaze.

How anguished was the waiting spell
      Of horror and of pain!
Then—then from out that fiery hell
      He staggered forth again:
The babe was safe, in blankets wrapt,
      The man flame lapt.

His record was an evil one,
      Of violence and sin.
No good on earth he'd ever done,
      Yet—may he Heaven win!
A gangster he . . . Is it not odd?
      —With guts of God.

SENSITIVE BURGLAR

Selecting in the dining-room
    The silver of his choice,
The burglar heard from chamber gloom
    A female voice.
As cold and bitter as a toad,
    She spat a nasty name,
So even as his swag he stowed
    He blushed for shame.

'You dirty dog!' he heard her say,
    'I sniff your whisky stench.
I bet you've gambled half your pay,
    Or blown it on a wench.
Begone from here, you rakehell boor!
    You shame the human race.
What wife would pillow-share with your
    Disgusting face!'

A tear the tender burglar shed,
    Then indignation rose,
And swiftly striding to her bed
    He said: 'I'm none of those.
I am a connoisseur in crime
    And felonies I plan . . .
But otherwise, believe me I'm
    A GENTLEMAN.'

THE PRISONER

Upspoke the culprit at the bar,
        Conducting his own case:
'Your Lordship, I have gone too far,
        But grant of me your grace.
As I was passing by a shop
        I saw my arm go out,
And though I begged of it to stop,
        It *stole* beyond a doubt.

'But why should my whole body be
        Condemned to dungeon grim,
For what in fact was only the
        Transgression of a limb?
So here before the Court I stand,
        And beg in Justice' name:
Please penalise my arm and hand,
        But not my frame.'

Outspoke the Judge with voice of ice,
        Although a smile he hid:
'Quite right! You should not pay the price
        For what one member did.
Your reasoning I must admit;
        Your arm should gaol expect . . .
Three months! And if you follow it
        The Court does not object.'

The culprit smiled with sudden charm,
  Then to the Court's dismay,
Quickly removed a wooden arm
    And went away.

GENTLE GAOLER

Being a gaoler I'm supposed
      To be a hard-boiled guy;
Yet never prison walls enclosed
      A kinder soul than I:
Passing my charges precious pills
      To end their ills.

And if in gentle sleep they die,
      And pass to pleasant peace,
No one suspects that it is I
      Who gave them their release:
No matter what the Doctor thinks,
      The Warden winks.

A lifer's is a fearful fate;
      It wrings the heart of me.
And what a saving to the State
      A sudden death must be!
Doomed men should have the legal right
      To end their plight.

And so my veronel they take,
      And bid goodbye to pain;
And sleep, and never, never wake
      To living hell again:
Oh call me curst or call me blest,—
      I give them rest.

GANGRENE

So often in the mid of night
  I wake me in my bed
With utter panic of affright
  To find my feet are dead;
And pace the floor to easy my pain
  And make them live again.

The folks at home are so discreet;
  They see me walk and walk
To keep the blood-flow in my feet,
  And though they never talk
I've heard them whisper: 'Mother may
  Have them *cut off* some day.'

Cut off my feet! I'd rather die . . .
  And yet the years of pain,
When in the darkness I will lie
  And pray to God in vain,
Thinking in agony: Oh why
Can doctors not annul our breath
  In honourable death?

THE AFFLICTED

Softly every night they come
            To the picture show,
That old couple, *deaf and dumb*
            In the second row;
Wistful watching, hand in hand,
            Proud they understand.

Shut-ins from the world away,
            All in all to each;
Knowing utter joy as they
            Read the lips of speech . . .
Would, I wonder, I be glum
            Were I deaf and dumb?

Were I quieted away,
            Far from din and shock?
Were I spared the need to say
            Silly things in talk?
Utter hush I would not mind . . .
            Happy they!—I'm *blind*.

POOR KID

Mumsie and Dad are raven dark
    And I am lily blonde.
' 'Tis strange,' I once heard nurse remark,
    'You do not correspond.'
And yet they claim me as their own,
    Born of their flesh and bone.

To doubt their parenthood I dread,
    But now to girlhood grown,
The thought is haunting in my head
    That I am *not* their own:
If so, my radiant bloom of youth
    Would wither in the truth.

'Twould give me anguish deep to know
    A fondling babe was I;
And that a maid in wedless woe
    Left me to live or die:
I'd rather Mother lied and lied
    To save my pride.

I love them both and they love me;
    I am their all, they say.
Yet though the sweetest home have we,
    To know I'm *theirs* I pray.
If not, please dear ones, never tell . . .
    The truth would be of hell.

CONFETTI IN THE WIND

He wrote a letter in his mind
    To answer one a maid had sent;
He sought the fitting word to find,
    As on by hill and rill he went.
By bluebell wood and hawthorn lane,
    The cadence sweet and silken phrase
He incubated in his brain
    For days and days.

He wrote his letter on a page
    Of paper with a satin grain;
It did not ring, so in a rage
    He tore it up and tried again.
Time after time he drafted it;
    He polished it all through the night;
He tuned and pruned till bit by bit
    He got it right.

He took his letter to the post,
    Yet long he held it in his hand.
Strangely his mood had veered, almost
    Reversed,—he could not understand.
The girl was vague, the words were vain;
    April romance had come to grief . . .
He tore his letter up again,—
    Oh blest relief!

THE CONTRAST

Fat lady, in your four-wheeled chair,
      Dolled up to beat the band,
At me you arrogantly stare
      With gold lorgnette in hand.
Oh how you differ from the dame
      So shabby, gaunt and grey,
With legs rheumatically lame,
      Who steers you on your way.

Nay, jewelled lady, look not back
      Lest you should be disturbed
To see the skinny hag in black
      Who boosts you up the curb.
Of course I know you get her cheap,
      Since she's a lady too,
And bite to eat and bed to sleep
      Maybe are all her due.

Alas for those who give us aid
      Yet need more help than we!
And though she thinks the wages paid
      Are almost charity,
I'd love to see that lady fat
      Lug round that hefty chair,
While with lorgnette and feathered hat
      Her handmaid lounges there.

BIRD WATCHER

In Wall Street once a potent power,
    And now a multi-millionaire
Alone within a shady bower
    In clothes his valet would not wear,
He watches bird wings bright the air.

The man who mighty mergers planned,
    And oil and coal kinglike controlled,
With field-glasses in failing hand
    Spies downy nestlings five days old,
With joy he could not buy for gold.

Aye, even childlike is his glee;
    But how he crisps with hate and dread
And shakes a clawlike fist to see
    A kestrel hover overhead:
Though he would never shoot it dead.

Although his cook afar doth forage
    For food to woo his appetite,
The old man lives on milk and porridge
    And now it is his last delight
At eve if one lone linnet lingers
    To pick crushed almonds from his fingers.

MY ANCESTORS

A barefoot boy I went to school
    To save a cobbler's fee,
For though the porridge pot was full
    A frugal folk were we;
We baked our bannocks, spun our wool,
    And counted each bawbee.

We reft our living from the soil,
    And I was shieling bred;
My father's hands were warped with toil,
    And crooked with grace he said.
My mother made the kettle boil
    As spinning wheel she fed.

My granny smoked a pipe of clay,
    And yammered of her youth;
The hairs upon her chin were grey,
    She had a single tooth;
Her mutch was grimed, I grieve to say,
    For I would speak the truth.

You of your ancestry may boast,—
    Well, here I brag of mine;
For if there is a heaven host
    I hope they'll be in line:
My dad with collie at his heel
    In plaid of tartan stripe;
My mammie with her spinning wheel,
    My granny with her pipe.

LONGEVITY

Said Brown: 'I can't afford to die
   For I have bought annuity,
And every day of living I
   Have money coming in to me:
While others toil to make their bread
   I make mine by not being dead.'

Said Jones: 'I can't afford to die,
   For I have books and books to write.
I do not care for pelf but I
   Would versify my visions bright;
Emotions noble in my breast
   By worthy words should be expressed.'

Said Smith: 'I can't afford to die,
   Because my life is kindly planned;
So many on my care rely,
   For comfort and a helping hand.
Too many weak ones need me so,
   And will be woeful when I go.'

Then Death appraisingly looked down,
   Saying: 'Your time's up, Mister Brown.
And I am sorry, Mister Jones,
   The earth is ready for your bones.
Friend Smith, although you're overdue
   Your lease of living we'll renew . . .
Both fame and fortune far above,
   What matters in the end is—Love.'

CAREERS

I knew three sisters,—all were sweet;
    Wishful to wed was I,
And wondered which would mostly meet
    The matrimonial tie.
I asked the first what fate would she
    Wish joy of life to bring her.
She answered: 'I would like to be
    A concert singer.'

I asked the second, for my mind
    Was set on nuptial noosing,
Unto what lot was she inclined
    If she could have the choosing?
Said she: 'For woman I can see
    No fortune finer,
Than to go in for Art and be
    A dress designer.'

With heavy heart I asked the third
    What was her life ambition;
A maiden she in look and word
    Of modest disposition.
'Alas, I dearly wish,' said she,
    'My aims were deeper:
My highest hope it is to be
    A good house-keeper.'

322

Which did I choose? Look at my home,—
     The answer's there;
As neat and sweet as honeycomb,
     With children fair.
And so it humbly seems to me,
     In common life,
A woman's glory is to be
     A good house-wife.

THE DECISION

Said she: 'Although my husband Jim
    Is with his home content,
I never should have married him,
    We are so different.
Oh yes, I know he loves me well,
    Our children he adores;
But he's so dull, and I rebel
    Against a life that bores.

'Of course there is another man,
    Quite pennyless is he;
And yet with hope and joy we plan
    A home beyond the sea.
Though I forfeit the name of wife
    And neighbours ostracise,
Such happiness will crown our life
    Their censure we'll despise.

'But then what will my children think,
    Whose love is pure and true?'
Said I: 'Your memory will stink
    If they should speak of you.
Your doting Jim will curse your name,
    And if you make a mess
Of life, oh do not in your shame
    Dare hope for happiness.'

Well, still with Jim she lives serene,
     And has of kiddies three.
'Oh what a fool I might have been
     To leave my home,' says she.
'Of course Jim is a priceless bore,
     But he's so sweet to me . . .
Come darling, won't you let me pour
     Another cup of tea?'

SPARTAN MOTHER

My mother loved her horses and
      Her hounds of pedigree;
She did not kiss the baby hand
      I held to her in glee.
Of course I had a sweet *nou-nou*
      Who tended me with care,
And mother reined her nag to view
      Me with a critic air.

So I went to a famous school,
      But holidays were short;
My mother thought me just a fool,
      Unfit for games and sport.
For I was fond of books and art,
      And hated hound and steed:
Said Mother, 'Boy, you break my heart!
      You are not of our breed.'

Then came the War. The Mater said:
      'Thank God, a son I give
To King and Country,'—well, I'm *dead*
      Who would have loved to live.
'For England's sake,' said she, 'he died.
      For that my boy I bore.'
And now she talks of me with pride,
      A hero of the War.

326

Mother, I think that you are glad
      I ended up that way.
Your horses and your dogs you had,
      And still you have today.
Your only child you say *you* gave
      Your Country to defend . . .
Dear Mother, from a hero's grave
      I—curse you in the end.

AT THE GOLDEN PIG

Where once with lads I scoffed my beer
 The landlord's lass I've wed.
Now I am lord and master here;—
 Thank God! the old man's dead.
I stand behind a blooming bar
 With belly like a tub,
And pals say, seeing my cigar:
  'Bill's wed a pub.'

I wonder now if I did well,
 My freedom for to lose;
Knowing my wife is fly as hell
 I mind my 'Ps' and 'Qs'.
Oh what a fuss she made because
 I tweaked the barmaid's bub:
Alas! a sorry day it was
  I wed a pub.

Fat landlord of the Golden Pig,
 They call me 'mister' now;
And many a mug of beer I swig,
 Yet don't get gay, somehow.
So farmer fellows, lean and clean
 Who sweat to earn your grub,
Although you haven't got a bean:
  Don't wed a pub.

FLORRIE

Because I was a wanton wild
    And welcomed many a lover,
Who is the father of my child
    I wish I could discover.
For though I know it is not right
    In tender arms to tarry,
A barmaid has to be polite
    To Tom and Dick and Harry.

My truest love was Poacher Jim:
    I wish my babe was his'n.
Yet I can't father it on him
    Because he was in prison.
As uniforms I like, I had
    A soldier and a sailor;
Then there was Pete the painter lad,
    And Timothy the tailor.

Though virtue hurt you vice ain't nice;
    They say to err is human;
Alas! one pays a bitter price,
    It's hell to be a woman.
Oh dear! Why was I born a lass
    Who hated to say: No, sir.
I'd better in my sorry pass
    Blame Mister Simms, the grocer.

HORATIO

His portrait hung upon the wall.
  Oh how at us he used to stare.
Each Sunday when I made my call! —
  And when one day it wasn't there,
Quite quick I seemed to understand
  The light was green to hold her hand.

Her eyes were amorously lit;
  I knew she wouldn't mind at all.
Yet what I did was sit and sit
  Seeing that blankness on the wall . . .
Horatio had a gentle face,—
  How would my mug look in his place?

That oblong of wall-paper wan!
  And while she prattled prettily
I sensed the *red* light going on,
  So I refused a cup of tea,
And took my gold-topped cane and hat—
  My going seemed to leave her flat.

Horatio was a decent guy,
    And when she ravished from her heart
A damsite better man than I,
    She seemed to me,—well, just a tart:
Her lack of tact I can't explain.
    His picture,—is it hung again?

RHYMES FOR RESIGNATION

CLEMENCEAU

His frown brought terror to his foes,
　　But now in twilight of his days
The pure perfection of a rose
　　Can kindle rapture in his gaze.
Where once he swung the sword of wrath
　　And peoples trembled at his word,
With hoe he trims a pansied path
　　　　And listens to a bird.

His large of life was lived with noise,
　　With war and strife and crash of kings:
But now he hungers for the joys
　　Of peace, and hush of homely things.
His old dog nuzzles by his knee,
　　And seems to say: 'Oh Master dear,
Please do not ever part from me!
　　　　We are so happy here.'

His ancient maid, as sky draws dim,
　　Calls to him that the soup grows cold.
She tyrannises over him
　　Who once held armies in his hold.
With slippers, old skull-cap and shawl
　　He dreams and dozes by the fire,
Sighing: 'Behold the end of all,
　　　　Sweet rest my sole desire.

'My task is done, my pen is still;
    My Book is there for all to see,—
The final triumph of my will,
    Ineffably, my victory.
A Tiger once, but now a lamb,
    With frailing hand my gate I close.
How hushed my heart! My life how calm!
            —Its crown a Rose.'

MISTINGUETTE

He was my one and only love;
My world was mirror for his face.
We were as close as hand and glove,
Until he came with smiling grace
To say: 'We must be wise, my dear.
You are the idol of today,
But I too plan a proud career,—
Let's kiss and go our way.'

And then he soared to sudden fame,
And even queens applauded him.
A halo glorified his name
That dust of time may never dim.
And me,—I toured golden Brazil,
Yet as gay mobs were cheering me,
The sun seemed black, the brilliance chill,
My triumph mockery.

Today if I should say: 'Hello!'
He'd say: 'How are you?' I'd say: 'Fine.'
Yet never shall he see the woe,
The wanness of my frail decline.
I love him now and always will.'
Oh may his star be long to set!
My Maurice is an idol still,—
What wreaths for Mistinguette!

ERNIE PYLE

I wish I had the simple style
  In writing verse,
As in his prose had Ernie Pyle,
  So true and terse;
Springing so forthright from the heart
  With guileless art.

I wish I could put back a dram
  As Ernie could;
I wish that I could cuss and damn
  As soldier should;
And fain with every verse would I
  Ernie outvie.

Alas! I cannot claim his high
  Humanity;
Nor emulate his pungent, dry
  Profanity;
Nor share his love of common folk
  Who bear life's yolk.

Oh Ernie, who on earth I knew
  In war and wine,
Though frail of frame, in soul how you
  Were pure and fine!
I'm proud that once when we were plastered
  You called me 'bastard.'

EINSTEIN

A little mousey man he was
    With board, and chalk in hand;
And millions were awestruck because
    They couldn't understand.
Said he: 'E equals Mc 2:
        I'll prove it true.'

No doubt you can, your marvel man,
    But will it serve our good?
Will it prolong our living span
    And multiply our food?
Will it bring peace between the nations
        To make equations?

Our thanks are due no doubt to you
    For truth beyond our ken;
But after all what did you do
    To ease the lot of men?
How can a thousand 'yous' be priced
        Beside a Christ?

TOM PAINE

An Englishman was Thomas Paine
    Who bled for liberty;
But while his fight was far from vain
    He died in poverty:
Though some are of the sober thinking
    'Twas due to drinking.

Yet this is what appeals to me:
    Cobbet, a friend, loved him so well
He sailed across the surly sea
    To raw and rigid New Rochelle:
With none to say: 'Take him not from us!'
    He raped the grave of Thomas.

And in his library he set
    These bones so woe-begone;
I have no doubt his eyes were wet
    To scan that skeleton.
That grinning scull from which in season
    Emerged the *Age of Reason*.

Then Cobbet in his turn lay dead,
    And auctioneering tones
Over his chattels rudely said:
    'Who wants them bloody bones?'
None did, so they were scattered far
    And God knows where they are.

A friend of Franklin and of Pitt
        He lived a stormy span;
The flame of liberty he lit
        And rang the Rights of Man.
Yet pilgrims from Vermont and Maine
In hero worship seek in vain
        The bones of Thomas Paine.

DYLAN

And is it not a gesture grand
    To drink oneself to death?
Oh sure 'tis I can understand,
    Being of sober breath.
And so I do not sing success,
    But dirge the damned who fall,
And who contempt for life express
    Through alcohol.

Of Stephen Foster and of Poe,
    Of Burns and Wilde I think;
And weary men who dared to go
    The wanton way of drink.
Strange mortals blind to bitter blame,
    And deaf to loud delight,
Who from the shades of sin and shame
    Enstar our night.

Among those dupes of destiny
    Add D.T. to my list,
Although his verse you may agree
    Leaves one in mental mist . . .
Oh ye mad poets, loth of life,
    Who peace in death divine,
Pass not by pistol, poison, knife,—
    Drown, drown in wine!

A CANVAS FOR A CRUST

Aye, Montecelli, that's the name.
You may have heard of him perhaps.
Yet though he never savoured fame,
Of those impressionistic chaps,
Monet and Manet and Renoir
      He was the avatar.

He festered in a Marseilles slum,
A starving genius, god-inspired.
You'd take him for a lousy bum,
Tho' poetry of paint he lyred,
In dreamy pastels each a gem: . . .
      How people laughed at them!

He peddled paint from bar to bar;
From sordid rags a jewel shone,
A glow of joy and colour far
From filth of fortune woe-begone.
'Just twenty francs,' he shyly said,
      'To take me drunk to bed.'

Of Van Gogh and Cezanne a peer;
In dreams of ecstasy enskied,
A genius and a pioneer,
Poor, paralysed and mad he died:
Yet by all who hold Beauty dear
      May he be glorified!

BENJAMIN FRANKLIN

Franklin fathered bastards fourteen,
  (So I read in the *New Yorker*);
If it's true, in terms of courtin'
  Benny must have been a corker.
To be prudent I've aspired,
  And my passions I have mastered;
So that I have never sired
    A single bastard.

One of course can never know;
  But I think that if I had
It would give me quite a glow
  When a kiddie called me 'Dad.'
Watching toddlers at their play,
  Parentage I'd gladly claim,
But their mothers smiling say:
      'You're not to blame.'

Ben founded the *Satevepost,*
  And for that I much respect him;
But fourteen is quite a host
  Paternally to elect him.
'Fatherhood is not a crime,'
  Deemed fat Ben, 'there *could* be others . . .
Darlings, I had not the time
      To wed your mothers.'

344

THE SEED

I was a seed that fell
    In silver dew;
And nobody could tell,
    For no one knew;
No one could tell my fate,
    As I grew tall;
None visioned me with hate,
    No, none at all.

A sapling I became,
    Blest by the sun;
No rumour of my shame
    Had any one.
Oh I was proud indeed,
    And sang with glee,
When from a tiny seed
    I grew a tree.

I was so stout and strong
    Though still so young,
When sudden came a throng
    With angry tongue;
They cleft me to the core
    With savage blows,
And from their ranks a roar
    Of rage arose.

I was so proud a seed
  A tree to grow;
Surely there was no need
  To lay me low.
Why did I end so ill,
  The midst of three
Black crosses on a hill
  Called Calvary?

STUPIDITY

Stupidity, woe's anodyne,
Be kind and comfort me in mine;
Smooth out the furrows of my brow,
Make me as carefree as a cow,
Content to sleep and eat and drink
        And never think.

Stupidity, let me be blind
To all the ills of humankind;
Fill me with simple sentiment
To walk the way my father went;
School me to sweat with robot folk
        Beneath the yoke.

Stupidity, keep in their place
The moiling masses of my race,
And bid the lowly multitude
Be humble as a people should;
Learn us with patient hearts, I pray,
        Lords to obey.

Stupidity and Ignorance,
Be you our buffers 'mid mischance;
Endoctrine us to do your will,
And other stupid people kill;
Fool us with hope of Life to be,
Great god to whom we bow the knee,
                    —STUPIDITY.

THE AFTERMATH

Although my blood I've shed
    In war's red wrath,
Oh how I darkly dread
    Its aftermath!
Oh how I fear the day
    Of my release,
When I must face the fray
    Of phoney peace!

When I must fend again
    In labour strife;
And toil with sweat and strain
    For kids and wife.
The world is so upset
    I battled for,
That grimly I regret
    The peace of war.

The wounds are hard to heal
    Of shell and shard,
But O the way to weal
    Is bitter hard!
Though looking back I see
    A gory path,
How bloody black can be
    War's Aftermath!

LITTLE BROTHER

Wars have been and wars will be
Till the human race is run;
Battles red by land and sea,
Never peace beneath the sun.
I am old and little care;
I'll be cold, my lips be dumb:
Brother mine, beware, beware . . .
Evil looms the wrath to come.

Eastern skies are dark with strife,
Western lands are stark with fear;
Rumours of world-war are rife,
Armageddon draweth near.
If your carcase you would save,
Hear, oh hear, the dreadful drum!
Fly to forest, cower in cave . . .
Brother, heed the wrath to come!

Brother, you were born too late;
Human life is but a breath.
Men delve deep, where darkly wait
Sinister the seeds of death,
There's no moment to delay;
Sorrowing the stars are blind.
Little Brother, how I pray
You may sanctuary find.
Peoples of the world succumb . . .
Fly, poor fools, the WRATH TO COME!

AT THE PARADE

I cannot flap a flag
     Or beat a drum;
Behind the mob I lag
     With larynx dumb;
Alas! I fear I'm not
     A Patriot.

With acrid eyes I see
     The soul of things;
And equal unto me
     Are cooks and kings;
I would not cross the street
     A duke to meet.

Oh curse me for a fool
     To be so proud;
To stand so still and cool
     Amid the crowd.
For President or Peer
     God, let me cheer!

But no, despite the glee
     My heart is cold;
I think that it may be
     Because I'm old;
I'm dumb where millions yell . . .
     Oh what the hell!

COMPASSION

What puts me in a rage is
The sight of cursed cages
Where singers of the sky
Perch hop instead of fly;
Where lions to and fro
Pace seven yards or so:
I who love space of stars
Have hate of bars.

I wince to see dogs chained,
Or horses bit restrained;
Or men of feeble mind
In straight-jackets confined;
Or convicts in black cells
Enduring earthly hells:
To me not to be free
Is fiendish cruelty.

To me not to be kind
Is evil of the mind.
No need to pray or preach,
Let us our children teach
With every fond caress
Pity and gentleness:
So in the end may we
God's Kingdom bring to be.

MY ROOM

I think the things I own and love
    Acquire a sense of me,
That gives them value far above
    The worth that others see.
My chattels are of me a part:
    This chair on which I sit
Would break its overstuffed old heart
    If I made junk of it.

To humble needs with which I live,
    My books, my desk, my bed,
A personality I give
    They'll lose when I am dead.
Sometimes on entering my room
    They look at me with fear,
As if they had a sense of doom
    Inevitably near.

Yet haply, since they do not die,
    In them will linger on
Some of the spirit that was I,
    When I am gone.
And maybe some sweet soul will sigh,
    And stroke with tender touch
The things I loved, and even cry
    A little,—not too much.

SAILOR SON

When you come home I'll not be round
        To welcome you.
They'll take you to a grassy mound
        So neat and new;
Where I'll be sleeping—O so sound!
        The ages through.

I'll not be round to broom the hearth,
        To feed the chicks;
And in the wee room of your birth
        Your bed to fix;
Rose room that knew your baby mirth
        Your tiny tricks.

I'll not be round . . . The garden still
        With bees will hum;
To cheerful you the throstle's bill
        Will not be dumb;
The rambler rose will overspill
        When you will come.

Bird, bee and bloom, they'll greet you all
        With scented sound;
Yet though the joy of your footfall
        Will thrill the ground
Your mother with her old grey shawl—
        Will not be round.

355

DEDICATION

In youth I longed to paint
    The loveliness I saw;
And yet by dire constraint
    I had to study Law.
But now all that is past,
    And I have no regret,
For I am free at last
        Law to forget.

To beauty newly born
    With brush and tube I play;
And though my daubs you scorn,
    I'll learn to paint some day.
When I am eighty old,
    Maybe I'll better them,
And you may yet behold
        A gem.

Old Renoir used to paint,
    Brush strapped to palsied hand;
His fervour of a saint
    How I can understand.
My joy is my reward,
    And though you gently smile,
Grant me to fumble, Lord,
        A little while!

TICK-TOCK

Tick-tocking in my ear
My dollar clock I hear.
'Arise,' it seems to say:
'Behold another day
To grasp the golden key
Of Opportunity;
To turn the magic lock—
          Tick-tock!

'Another day to gain
Some goal you sought in vain;
To sing a sweeter song,
Perchance to right a wrong;
To win a height unscaled
Where yesterday you failed;
To brave a battle shock—
          Tick-tock!'

You measure out my breath,
Each beat one nearer death . . .
O God, grant unto me
A few more years to be,
That somehow I may prove
My loyalty and love:
Wind up this worn-out clock,
          Tick-tock,
          Tick-tock!

AT EIGHTY YEARS

As nothingness draws near
How I can see
Inexorably clear
My vanity.
My sum of worthiness
Always so small,
Dwindles from less to less
To none at all.

As grisly destiny
Claims me at last,
How grievous seem to me
Sins of my past!
How keen a conscience edge
Can come to be!
How pitiless the dredge
Of memory!

Ye proud ones of the earth
Who count your gains,
What cherish you of worth
For all your pains?
E'er death shall slam the door,
Will you, like me,
Face fate and count the score—
FUTILITY.

SEVEN

If on water and sweet bread
Seven years I'll add to life,
For me will no blood be shed,
No lamb know the evil knife;
Excellently will I dine
On a crust and Adam's wine.

If a bed in monkish cell
Will mean old of age to me,
Let me in a convent dwell,
And from fellow men be free;
Let my mellow sunset days
Pass in piety and praise.

For I love each hour I live,
Wishing it were twice as long;
Dawn my gratitude I give,
Laud the Lord with evensong:
Now that moons are sadly few
How I grudge the grave its due!

Yet somehow I seem to know
Seven Springs are left to me;
Seven Mays may cherry tree
Will allume with sudden snow . . .
Then let seven candles shine
Silver peace above my shrine.

SEA SORCERY

Oh how I love the laughing sea,
  Sun lances splintering;
Or with a virile harmony
  In salty caves to sing;
Or mumbling pebbles on the shore,
  Or roused to monster might:
By day I love the sea, but more
  I love it in the night.

High over ocean hangs my home
  And when the moon is clear
I stare and stare till fairy foam
  Is music in my ear;
Till glamour dances to a tune
  No mortal man could make;
And there bewitched beneath the moon
  To beauty I awake.

Then though I seek my bed again
  And close the shutters tight,
Still, still I hear that wild refrain
  And see that mystic light . . .
Oh reckon me a crazy loon,
  But blessèd I will be
If my last seeing be the moon,
  My last sound—the Sea.

360

O LOVELY LIE

I told a truth, a tragic truth
    That tore the sullen sky;
A million shuddered at my sooth
    And anarchist was I.
Red righteousness was in my word
    To winnow evil chaff;
Yet while I swung crusading sword
    I heard the devil laugh.

I framed a lie, a rainbow lie
    To glorify a thought;
And none was so surprise as I
    When fast as fire it caught.
Like honey people lapped my lie
    And peddled it abroad,
Till in a lift of sunny sky
    I saw the smile of God.

If falsehood may be best, I thought,
    To hell with verity;
Dark truth may be a cancer spot
    'Twere better not to see.
Aye, let a lie be big and bold
    Yet ripe with hope and ruth,
Beshrew me! but its heart may hold
    More virtue than the truth.

THE PALACE

Grimy men with picks and shovels
　　Who in darkness sweat unseen,
Climb from out your lousy hovels,
　　Build a palace for the Queen;
Praise the powers that be for giving
　　You a chance to make a living.

Yet it would be better far
　　Could you build with cosy lure
Skyey tenements where are
　　Rabbit-warrens of the poor;
With a hope bright as a gem
　　Some day you might live in them.

Could the Queen just say: 'A score
　　Of rich palaces have I.
Do not make me any more,—
　　Raise a hostel heaven-high;
House the hundreds who have need,
　　To their misery give heed.'

Could she make this gesture fine
　　To the pit where labour grovels,
Mother hearts would cease to pine,
　　Weary men would wave their shovels.
All would cry with hope serene:
　　'Little children, bless the Queen!'

ORPHAN SCHOOL

Full fifty merry maids I heard
      One summer morn a-singing;
And each was like a joyous bird
      With spring-clear note a-ringing.
It was an old-time soldier song
      That held their happy voices:
Oh how it's good to swing along
      When youth rejoices!

Then lo! I dreamed long years had gone,
      They passed again ungladly.
Their backs were bent, their cheeks were wan,
      Their eyes were staring sadly.
Their ranks were thinned by full a score
      From death's remorseless reaping;
Their steps were slow, they sang no more,—
      Nay, some were weeping.

Dark dream! I saw my maids today
      Singing so innocently;
Their eyes with happiness were gay,
      They looked at me so gently.
Thought I: Be merry in your youth
      With hearts unrueing:
Thank God you do not know the truth
      Of Life's Undoing!

JOEY

I thought I would go daft when Joey died.
He was my first, and wise beyond his years.
For nigh a hundred nights I cried and cried,
Until my weary eyes burned up my tears.
Willie and Rosie tried to comfort me:
A woeful, weeping family were we.

I was a widow with no friends at all,
Ironing men's shirts to buy my kiddies grub;
And then one day a lawyer came to call,
Me with my arms deep in the washing-tub.
The gentleman who ran poor Joey down
Was willing to give us a thousand poun'.

What a godsend! It meant goodbye to care,
The fear of being dumped out on the street.
Rosie and Willie could have wool to wear,
And more than bread and margerine to eat . . .
To Joey's broken little legs we owe
Our rescue from a fate of want and woe.

How happily he hurried home to me,
Bringing a new-baked, crisp-brown loaf of bread.
The headlights of the car he did not see,
And when help came they thought that he was dead.
He stared with wonder from a face so wan . . .
A long, last look and he was gone,—was gone.

We've comfort now, and yet it hurts to know
We owe our joy to little, laughing Joe.

SONGS FOR SERENITY

SYMPATHY

My Muse is simple,—yet it's nice
To think you don't need to think twice
       On words I write.
I reckon I've a common touch
And if you say I cuss too much
       I answer: 'Quite!'

I envy not the poet's lot;
He has something I haven't got,
       Alas, I know.
But I have something maybe he
Would envy just a mite in me,—
       I'm rather *low*.

For I am cast of common clay,
And from a ditch I fought my way,
       And that is why
The while the poet scans the skies,
My gaze is grimly gutterwise,
       Earthy am I.

And yet I have a gift, perhaps
Denied to proud poetic chaps
       Who scoff at me;
I know the hearts of humble folk;
I too have bowed beneath the yoke:
So let my verse for them evoke
       Your sympathy.

MY CHAPEL

In idle dream with pipe in hand
    I looked across the Square,
And saw the little chapel stand
    In eloquent despair.
A ruin of the War it was,
    A dreary, dingy mess:
It worried me a lot because
    My hobby's happiness.

The shabby Priest said: 'You are kind.
    Time leaves us on the lurch,
And there are very few who mind
    Their duty to the Church.
But with this precious sum you give,
    I'll make it like a gem;
Poor folks will come, our altar live
    To comfort them.'

So now my chapel of despair
    Is full of joy and song;
I watch the humble go to prayer
    Although I don't belong.
An artist and agnostic I
    Possess but little pelf;
But oh what blessings it can buy
    Them—and myself!

THE GOAT AND I

Each sunny day upon my way
    A goat I pass;
He has a beard of silver grey,
    A bell of brass.
And all the while I am in sight
    He seems to muse,
And stares at me with all his might
    And chews and chews.

Upon the hill so thymy sweet
    With joy of Spring,
He hails me with a tiny bleat
    Of welcoming.
Though half the globe is drenched with blood
    And cities flare,
Contentedly he chews the cud
    And does not care.

Oh gentle friend, I know not what
    Your age may be,
But of my years I'd give the lot
    Yet left to me,
To chew a thistle and not choke,
    But bright of eye
Gaze at the old world-weary bloke
    Who hobbles by.

Alas! though bards make verse sublime,
    And lines to quote,
It takes a fool like me to rhyme
    About a goat.

YOU AND ME

I'm part of people I have known
     And they are part of me;
The seeds of thought that I have sown
     In other minds I see.
There's something of me in the throne
     And in the gallows tree.

There's something of me in each one
     With whom I work and play,
For islanded there can be none
     In this dynamic day;
And meshed with me perchance may be
     A leper in Cathay.

There's me in you and you in me,
     For deeply in us delves
Such common thought that never we
     Can call ourselves ourselves.
In coils of universal fate
     No man is isolate.

For you and I are History,
     The all that ever was;
And woven in the tapestry
     Of everlasting laws,
Persist will we in Time to be,
     Forever you and me.

PERIODS

My destiny it is tonight
    To sit with pensive brow
Beside my study fire and write
    This verse I'm making now.
This Period, this tiny dot
    My pencil has defined,
By centuries of human thought
        Was predestined.

And my last period of all
    With patience now I see;
The final point so very small,
    That locks my life for me.
Yet in eternity of time
    They relatively seem
So like,—the dot that rounds my rhyme
        Or ends my dream.

For each was preordained by Fate
    Since human life began;
So are the little and the great
    Linked in the life of man.
And as I wait without heartache
    The pencil-point of God,
To pattern predestined I make
        This——.

WHEELS

Since I am sick of Wheels
       That jar my day,
Unto the hush that heals
       I steal away.
Unto the core of Peace
       Nature reveals,
I go to win release
       From Wheels.

Let me beneath the moon
       Take desert trail;
Or on some lost lagoon
       Serenely sail;
Win to some peak the grey
       Storm cloud conceals . . .
Life, let me get away
       From Wheels!

Why was I born so late?
       A skin-clad man
I should have shared the fate
       Of mountain clan;
My quiet flock beside,
       When silence steals,
Unshocked in eventide
       By Wheels.

The Wheel is King today,
      And speed's a god;
Yet when I see the way
      My feet have trod,
Like pilgrims who to shrine
      Of Beauty kneels,
I pray: O Peace divine
      Damn Wheels!

MY HUNDRED BOOKS

A thousand books my library
      Contains;
And all are primed, it seems to me,
      With brains.
Mine are so few I scratch in thought
      My head;
For just a hundred of the lot
      I've read.

A hundred books, but of the best,
      I can
With wisdom savour and digest
      And scan.
Yet when afar from kin and kith
      In nooks
Of quietness I'm happy with
      Sweet books.

So as nine hundred at me stare
      In vain,
My lack I'm wistfully aware
      Of brain;
Yet as my leave of living ends,
      With looks
Of love I view a hundred friends,
      My Books.

TWO WORDS

'God' is composed of letters three,
        But if you put an 'l'
Before the last it seems to me
        A synonym for Hell.
For all of envy, greed and hate
        The human heart can hold
Respond unto the devil's bait
        Of Gold.

When God created Gold to be
        For our adorning fit,
I little think he dreamed that we
        Would come to worship it.
But when you ruefully have scanned
        The chronicles of Time,
You'll find that lucre lends a hand
        To Crime.

So if you are a millionaire,
        To be of Heaven sure,
Give every penny you can spare
        Unto the sick and poor.
From Gold strike out the evil 'ell,'
        And so with letters odd
You can with peace of spirit spell
        Just GOD.

THE CHOICE

Some inherit manly beauty,
Some come into worldly wealth;
Some have lofty sense of duty,
Others boast exultant health.
Though the pick may be confusing,
Health, wealth, charm or character,
If you had the chance of choosing
  Which would you prefer?

I'm not sold on body beauty,
Though health I appreciate;
Character and sense of duty
I resign to Men of State.
I don't need a heap of money;
Oh I know I'm hard to please.
Though to you it may seem funny,
  I want none of these.

No, give me Imagination,
And the gift of weaving words
Into patterns of creation,
With the lilt of singing birds;
Passion and the power to show it,
Sense of life with love expressed:
Let me be a bloody poet,—
  You can keep the rest.

380

A MEDIOCRE MAN

I'm just a mediocre man
 Of no high-brow pretence;
A comfortable life I plan
 With care and commonsense.
I do the things most people do,
 I echo what they say;
And through my morning paper view
 The problems of the day.

No doubt you think I'm colourless,
 Profoundly commonplace;
And yet I fancy, more or less,
 I represent the race.
My name may stand for everyone,
 At least for nine in ten,
For all in all the world is run
 By mediocre men.

Of course you'll maybe not agree
 That *you* are average,
And unlike ordinary me
 You strut your little stage,
Well, you may even own a Bank,
 And mighty mergers plan,
But Brother, doff your tile and thank
 The Mediocre Man.

IMAGINATION

A gaunt and hoary slab of stone
    I found in desert space,
And wondered why it lay alone
    In that abandoned place.
Said I: 'Maybe a Palace stood
    Where now the lizards crawl,
With courts of musky quietude
    And turrets tall.

Maybe where low the vultures wing
    'Mid mosque and minaret,
The proud pavilion of a King
    Was luminously set.
'Mid fairy fountains, alcoves dim,
    Upon a garnet throne
He ruled,—and now all trace of him
    Is just this stone.

Ah well, I've done with wandering,
    But from a blousy bar
I see with drunk imagining
    A Palace like a star.
I build it up from one grey stone
    With gardens hanging high,
And dream . . . Long, long ere Babylon
    Its King was I.

TO A STUFFED SHIRT

On the tide you ride head high,
Like a whale 'mid little fishes;
I should envy you as I
Help my wife to wash the dishes.
Yet frock-coat and stove-pipe hat
Cannot hide your folds of fat.

You are reckoned a success,
And the public praise you win;
There's your picture in the Press,
Pouchy eyes and triple chin.
Wealth,—of it you fairly stink;
Health,—what does your Doctor think?

Dignity is phoney stuff.
Who is dignified deep down?
Strip the pants off, call the bluff,
Common clay are king and clown.
Let a bulging belly be
Your best bid for dignity.

Miserable millionaire!
For indulgence you must pay.
Yet there's salvation in prayer,—
Down on your fat knees and pray.
Know that with your dying breath
There is dignity in death.

WORDS

If on isle of the sea
     I have to tarry,
With *one* book, let it be
     A Dictionary.
For though I love life's scene,
     It seems absurd,
My greatest joy has been
     The printed word.

Though painter with delight
     May colours blend,
They are but in his sight
     Means to an end.
Yet while I harmonise
     Or pattern them,
A precious word I prize
     Like to a gem.

A fiddler lures fine tone
     From gut and wood;
A sculptor from stark stone
     Shapes godlihood.
But let me just caress,
     Like silver birds,
For their own loveliness—
     Bewitching words.

THE SEARCH

I bought a young and lovely bride,
    Paying her father gold;
Lamblike she rested by my side,
    As cold as ice is cold.
No love in her could I awake,
    Even for pity's sake.

I bought rich books I could not read,
    And pictures proud and rare;
Reproachfully they seemed to plead
    And hunger for my care;
But to their beauty I was blind,
    Even as is a hind.

The bearded merchants heard my cry:
    'I'll give all I possess
If only, only I can buy
    A little happiness.'
Alas! I sought without avail:
    They had not *that* for sale.

I gave my riches to the poor
    And dared the desert lone;
Now of God's heaven I am sure
    Though I am rag and bone . . .
Aye, richer than the Aga Khan,
    At last—a happy man.

TOURISTS

In a strange town in a far land
    They met amid a throng;
They stared, they could not understand
    How life was sudden song.
As brown eyes looked in eyes of grey
    Just for a moment's space,
Twin spirits met with sweet dismay
    In that strange place.

And then the mob that swept them near
    Reft them away again;
Two hearts in all the world most dear
    Knew puzzlement and pain.
They barely brushed in passing by,
    A wildered girl and boy,
Who should have clasped with laughing cry,
    And wept for joy.

But no, the crowd cleft them apart,
    And she went East, he West;
But there was havoc in his heart
    And brooding in her breast.
In a far land, in a strange town
    Amid a mob they met;
They stared, they passed . . . But O deep down,
    Can they forget?

THE ROBBERS

Alas! I see that thrushes three
 Are ravishing my old fig tree,
In whose green shade I smoked my pipe
 And waited for the fruit to ripe;
From green to purple softly swell
 Then drop into my lap to tell
That it is succulently sweet
 And excellent to eat.

And now I see the crimson streak,
 The greedy gash of yellow beak.
And look! the finches come in throng,
 In wavy passage, light with song;
Of course I could scare them away,
 But with a shrug: 'The heck!' I say.
I owe them something for their glee,
 So let them have their spree.

For all too soon in icy air
    My fig tree will be bleak and bare,
Until it wake from Winter sleep
    And button buds begin to peep.
Then broad leaves come to shelter me
    In luminous placidity.
Then figs will ripen with a rush
    And brash will come the thrush.

But what care I though birds destroy
My fruit,—they pay me back with joy.

MY VINEYARD

To me at night the stars are vocal.
They say: 'Your planet's oh so local!
A speck of dust in heaven's ceiling;
Your faith divine a foolish feeling.
What odds if you are chaos hurled,
Yours is a silly little world.'

For their derision, haply true,
I hate the stars, as wouldn't you?
But whether earth be great or little,
I do not care a fishwife's spittle;
I do not fret its where or why,—
Today's a day and I am I.

Serene, afar from woe and worry
I tend my vines and do not hurry.
I buss the lass and tip the bottle,
Fill up the glass and rinse my throttle.
Tomorrow though the earth should perish,
The lust of life today I cherish.

Ah no, the stars I will not curse:
Though things are bad they might be worse.
So when vast constellations shine
I drink to them in ruby wine;
For they themselves,—although it odd is,
Somehow give me a sense that God is.

Because we trust and realise
His love he steers us in the skies.
For faith however foolish can
Be mighty helpful to a man:
And as I tend my vines so He
With tenderness looks after me.

MY DOG'S MY BOSS

Each day when it's anighing three
      Old Dick looks at the clock,
Then proudly brings my stick to me
      To mind me of our walk.
And in his doggy rapture he
      Does everything but talk.

But since I lack his zip and zest
      My old bones often tire;
And so I ventured to suggest
      Today we hug the fire.
But with what wailing he expressed
      The death of his desire!

He gazed at me with eyes of woe
      As if to say: 'Old Boy,
You mustn't lose your grip, you know,
      Let us with laughing joy,
On heath and hill six miles or so
      Our legs and lungs employ.'

And then his bark stilled to a sigh
    He flopped upon the floor;
But such a soft old mug am I
    I threw awide the door;
So gaily, though the wind was high
    We hiked across the moor.

BREATH IS ENOUGH

I draw sweet air
Deeply and long,
As pure as prayer,
As sweet as song.
Where lilies glow
And roses wreath,
Heart-joy I know
Is just to breathe.

Aye, so I think
By shore or sea,
As deep I drink
Of purity.
This brave machine,
Bare to the buff,
I keep ice-clean,
Breath is enough.

From mountain stream
To covert cool
The world, I deem,
Is wonderful;
The great, the small,
The smooth, the rough,
I love it all,—
Breath is enough.

RIPENESS

With peace and rest
And wisdom sage,
Ripeness is best
Of every age.
With hands that fold
In pensive prayer,
For grave-yard mold
      Prepare.

From fighting free
With fear forgot,
Let ripeness be,
Before the rot.
With heart of cheer
At eighty odd,
How man grows near
      To God!

With passion spent
And life nigh run
Let us repent
The ill we've done.
And as we bless
With happy heart
Life's mellowness
      —Depart.

394

A CABBAGE PATCH

Folk ask if I'm alive,
      Most think I'm not;
Yet gaily I contrive
      To till my plot.
The world its way can go,
      I little heed,
So long as I can grow
      The grub I need.

For though long overdue,
      The years to me,
Have taught a lesson true,
      —Humility.
Such better men than I
      I've seen pass on;
Their pay-off when they die:
      —Oblivion.

And so I mock at fame,
      With books unread;
No monument I claim
      When I am dead;
Contented as I see
      My cottage thatch
That my last goal should be
      —A cabbage patch.

THE SCORE

I asked a silver sage
       With race nigh run:
'Tell me in old of age
       Your wisdom won?'
Said he: 'From fret and strife
       And vain vexation,
The all I've learned from life
       Is—Resignation.'

I asked a Bard who thrummed
       A harp clay-cold:
'How is your story summed
       Now you are old?'
Though golden voice was his,
       And fame had he,
He sighed: 'The finish is
       —Futility.'

I'm old; I have no wealth
       Toil to reward;
Yet for the boon of health
       I thank the Lord.
While Beauty I can see,
       To *live* is good;
And so life's crown to me
       Is—Gratitude.

WORK AND JOY

Each day I live I thank the Lord
     I do the work I love;
And in it find a rich reward,
     All price and praise above.
For few may do the work they love,
     The fond unique employ,
That fits them as a hand a glove,
     And gives them joy.

Oh gentlefolk, do you and you
     Who toil for daily hire,
Consider that the job you do
     Is to your heart's desire?
Aye, though you are to it resigned,
     And will no duty shirk,
Oh do you in your private mind
     Adore your work?

Twice happy man whose job is joy,
     Whose hand and heart combine,
In brave and excellent employ
     As radiantly as mine!
But oh the weary, dreary day,
     The wear and tear and irk
Of countless souls who cannot say:
     'I love my work.'

CONTENTMENT

Bed and bread are all I need
        In my happy day;
Love of Nature is my creed,
        Unto her I pray;
Sun and sky my spirit feed
        On my happy way.

To no man I bow the head,
        None may master me;
I will eat my crust of bread
        Lauding liberty;
And upon my truckle bed
        Glory to be free.

You who grab for sordid gold,
        You who fight for fame,
Shiny dross your fingers hold,
        Empty is your aim.
—Soon we fatten graveyard mould,
        Rich and poor the same.

So from world of want and woe
        I retreat with dread;
Tuned to Nature glad I go
        With my bite of bread:
Praising God I lay me low
        On my truckle bed.

THE PARTING

Sky's a-waxin' grey,
Got to be a-goin';
Gittin' on my way,
Where? I ain't a-knowin'.
Fellers, no more jokes,
Fun an' frisky greetin'—
So long, all you folks,
Been nice our meetin'.

Sky's a-growin' dark,
Have to be a-startin'.
Feeble is the spark,
Pitiful the partin'.
Family an' all,
Thanks for joy I owe you;
Gotta take my call;
Been sweet to know you.

Sky's a-mighty black,
Close my heart's to breakin'.
Lonesome is the track
I must now be takin'.
Lordy, be You nigh,
Now's my time to prove you . . .
Life, good-bye, good-bye,—
Been grand to love you!

L'ENVOI

Only a rhymer, so I am,
          Lone in the market place;
I shrink, and no one cares a damn
          Though tears corrode my face.
The hollows of my cheeks they track,
          Symbolic of vain hope;
My hands are grimed because I lack
          The price of soap.

Only a rhymer! How my breeks
          Let in the Winter wind;
One of my shoes obscenely leaks,
          My coat is safety pinned.
Although my neb drips bead on bead,
          No handkerchief have I;
My lips are blue, but none have heed
          My songs to buy.

Only a rhymer,—just a chiel
          Spewed from the land of Burns,
A wastrel and a ne'er-do-weel,
          From whom the public turns.
Alas! It is too late to mend
          The error of my ways,
So I will jingle to the end
          Of all my days.

BOOK THREE

VERSE FROM PROSE WRITINGS

IN THE LAND OF PALE-BLUE SNOW

In the land of pale-blue snow,
Where it's ninety-nine below,
And the polar bears are dancing on the plain,
Oh, my Heart, my Life, my Soul,
I will meet thee when the ice-worms nest again.

from 'The Trail of '98'

I SEE WITHIN MY TRUE LOVE'S EYES

I see within my true love's eyes
The wide blue spaces of the skies;
I see within my true love's face
The rose and lily vie in grace;
I hear within my true love's voice
The songsters of the Spring rejoice.
Oh, why need I seek Nature's charms?—
I hold my true love in my arms.

from 'The Trail of '98'
Lines on a gold-backed hand-mirror

404

PROCLAIM OUR FAITH WITH
RINGING CHEERS

Proclaim our faith with ringing cheers;
By trumpet let the truth be told:
A man may live a hundred years . . .
Let us grow young instead of old.

Oh, how I love to souse my throttle
With rich red wine from a dusty bottle:
Alas! my doctor says I oughter
Drink only tea and Vichy water.

I'd love to puff a panatella
With any other lusty fella;
Alas! if I should chance to wish one:
"Tabac's tabooed!" shrieks my physician.

from 'Why Not Grow Young?'

OF BOOKS AND SCRIBES THERE IS NO END

Of Books and Scribes there is no end:
This Plague—and who can doubt it?
Dismays me so, I've sadly penned
Another book about it.

Title page quotation from
First Edition of 'The Pretender'

ON QUITTING AMERICA

Grey sea, grey sea, and grey, so grey
The ragged roof-line of my home;
Yet greyer far my mood than they,
As here amid the spawn of Rome
With tenderness undreamt before
I sigh: "Adieu, my native shore!
To thee my wistful eyes I strain;
To thee, brave burg, I wave my hand;
Good-bye, oh giddy Tungsten Lane!
Good-bye, oh great Skyscraper Land!"

from 'The Pretender'

PEDLAR OF DREAM STUFF

Pedlar of dream stuff, piping an empty tune;
Fisher of shadows, Ploughman of the Moon.

Though names I change from time to time,
A stickler for correctness I'm.
To write God-honest truth I strive,
And here, to best of memory, I've.

Of my good deeds I never yet
Have grudged a single one;
But O how deeply I regret
Good deeds I *might* have done!

　　　　　from 'Ploughman of the Moon'
　　　　　—the first half of Service's autobiography

UNDER THE MOULD

(written after hearing a girl sing 'After the Ball')

After the fight is over
After the strife is done,
After the bells are pealing
After the triumph won;
What is life's scene of glory
When all the tale is told?—
A shroud and a feast for the blind worm
UNDER THE MOULD.

ALTHOUGH MY SUM OF YEARS MAY BE NIGH SEVENTY AND SEVEN

Although my sum of years may be
Nigh seventy and seven,
With eyes of ecstasy I see
And hear the Harps of Heaven

The hills of Hollywood look down
Upon the honky tonky town;
Serene, aloof, austere they brood
Above egregious Hollywood.

> *from* 'Harper of Heaven'
> ——the second half of Service's autobiography

408

JOHNNY WAYNE AND
RANDY SCOTT

Johnny Wayne and Randy Scott
They fought and fought and fought and fought
With joy they shed each other's gore,
And then they paused and shed some more.
To bust each other's blocks they strove;
They wrecked the bar and crashed the stove.
Then with a heave big Johnny Wayne
Hurled Randy through the window pane.
So in the street and down the lot
They fought and fought and fought and fought.
So fierce they mixed it up I'll bet
Them galoots might be fighting yet.

TO G.K.

Princess, whose magic pen was dipped
   In radiant colours of romance
To write the wonder of your script,
   Your fairy-tale of chance?

Bring us Beauty, Art and Grace
   Be welcome to this land of ours
And with our homage take your place
   'Mid song and flowers.

Long may you play your golden part,
   Not only to en-sky your name,
But to be throned in every heart
   With heart-fire fame.

A people we, proud of our Past,
   From modern urgency afar,
Long have we hoped with faith steadfast
   To hail with ecstasy a Star.

Sweet Princess, may our dream come true—
Our Star be You.

*The above poem was written by Service for the occasion
of the marriage of Prince Rainier of Monaco to Grace
Kelly.*

WE ARE A PEOPLE FEW
AND FAR AWAY

We are a people few and far away
   Little our lives are crystalled with delight
For through the sunshine of the long, long day
   Loometh the shadow of the long, long night.

You who have come and seen and gone away
   O may your memories of us be bright!
May your life-season be the long, long day
   Unhaunted by the shadow of the night.

*Service wrote the above on a copy of 'Songs of a Sour-
dough' which he presented. He dated the flyleaf 'Daw-
son, Y.S., 27th August, 1909'.*

BOOK FOUR

SELECTION FROM
UNPUBLISHED VERSE

VIGNETTES IN VERSE

I don't believe in all I write,
   But seek to give a point of view;
Am I unreasonable? Quite!
   I'm ready to agree with you . . .
Times, though opponents we deride,
   Let's try to see the other side.

CONTINENTAL TRAINS

World-famous trains my garden pass
    A dozen times a day;
Long and luxurious of class,
    Mid palms they push their way;
And some are bound for Italy,
    While some are sped for Spain;
And some for Berlin on the Spree,
    Or Paris on the Seine.

And as I watch them puff and pull
    My travel feet I feel;
They itch for Zurich and Stamboul,
    For Naples and Seville.
Sleek conjurers of bright desire,
    Of up-and-going pains,
Imagination fast to fire
    Are Continental trains.

The sleeping and the dining cars
    Superbly pass me by,
With richness that the pocket bars
    From scribblers such as I.
My garden where the roses foam
    With love I live amid,
But Oh! I dream of golden Rome,
    And glamorous Madrid.

Yet with my blanket on my back
  In youth I beat my way
Along a lousy railway track
  From Maine to Monterey.
Alas! What sybarites are we,
  As life's soft twilight wanes,
Who seek the scented luxury
  Of Continental trains!

CLASSES

Alas! the horde of humankind
    Exist in woe and strife;
They grovel in the grime to find
    Necessities of life:
Yet roof and raiment, fire and feed
    Are all their need.

The smug and snug white-collar class
    In which I have been born
Ignore the squalid labour mass
    Or look on them with scorn;
Suburban comfort is their goal,
    Security their soul.

The bloated wealthy of the world,
    Demand of life the best,
Serene in golden languor curled
    They reck not of the rest;
Unheeding of gaunt need they be
    And loll in luxury.

So as I go my middle way
    Between the hovelled ditch,
And lawns of loveliness that gay
    The mansions of the rich,
I wonder—will Man ever see
    Classless Society?

TWO WORLDS

When I was rising twenty-two
   And full of guts and grit,
I quit the Old World for the New,
   Saying: "To heck with it!"
Dull ways of safety and of ease
   I held with heart of scorn,
And sought beyond the senile seas
   A land new-born.

But now that New World for the Old
   I leave, for life has sped;
To find, though I've a heap of gold,
   My friends of youth are dead.
Their names are graved on granite stones,
   But lone for them am I;
So I have come to lay my bones
   Where loved ones lie.

For oh! the New World's brave and bright
   When one is young and bold;
But when aweary of the fight
   My heart aches for the Old.
I leave my life-work over there,
   Hoping 'tis not in vain . . .
But now,—thank God for all His care:
   I'll Home again.

THE MYSTERY

When God says: "Son, your time is up"
 You've had your show;
Your moment's come to drink the Cup,
 You've got to go.
Four score of years you've carried on,
 You can't complain;
So then back to oblivion
 You go again.

It's true I've almost run my course;
 Faint is the flame.
And I must go back to the source
 From which I came.
The what it is I do not know,
 Nor any one
Can tell me where that I will go
 When life is done.

So all will end in mystery,
 In vision vain;
The page of human history
 Will ne'er explain.
And that is just as it should be;
 Don't think it odd,—
If we could understand God He
 Would not be God.

IN PRAISE OF ALCOHOL

Of vintage wine I am a lover;
To drink deep would be my delight;
If 'twere not for the bleak hangover
I'd get me loaded every night;
I'd whoop it up with song and laughter—
If 'twere not for the morning after.

For though to soberness I'm given
It is a thought I've often thunk:
The nearest that is Earth to Heaven
Is to get sublimely drunk;
Is to achieve divine elation
By means of generous libation.

Alas, the wine-cups claim their payment
And as the price is often pain,
If we could sense what morning grey meant
We never would get soused again;
Rather than buy a hob-nailed liver
I'm sure that we'd abstain for ever.

Yet how I love the glow of liquor,
As joyfully I drink it up!
Hoping that unto life's last flicker
With praise I'll raise the ruby cup;
And let me like a jolly monk
Proceed to get sublimely drunk.

RHYME AND ME

Said I to Rhyme: "I'm sick of you,
To death you're sadly overdue.
I'm weary of your tinny chimes
I've struck more than ten thousand times.
And yet I know each stale refrain
I'll use again and yet again;
Or else, if desperate I be,
I'll take to making verse that's free.
But that's so easy to compose
I might as well be writing prose . . .
Ah, no! I guess I'll have to stick
To lines which have an end that click."

Said Rhyme to me: "Oh, Bard ungrate,
To me you owe your lucky fate.
And all you have and all you are,
Your yacht, your villa and your car.
Your wife's tiara and her mink
Are her's because your verses clink.
If you indulged in stanzas blank,
You'd have no money in the bank.
I reckon, Pal, your happy time
Is based upon the rock of Rhyme.
Despite your words so worn and stale
You dine on caviar and quail,"

Whereat I hung my head with shame,
Of brash banality to blame . . .
Yet go on jingling just the same.

THE TWENTY-FIFTH HOUR

My daily hours are twenty-five,
  (The last is fictive, I confess)
And yet in that I'm most alive,
  And touch my peak of happiness:
One exoteric moment I'm
  Outside of Time.

It mostly comes in dead of night,
  To wean me from the world away;
Or in the looming of the light,
  In loneliness at birth of day:
That Time extension comes to me,
  I know as Ecstasy.

Contentment crowns my common days,
  And Happiness in fee I hold,
While on the shining peak of praise
  The light of Joy is often gold:
But Ecstasy is known to few,—
  Oh, say, it come to you.

Not sourly dialled by the clock,
  Your hours be twenty-five;
One mystic moment. Time to mock,
  Transcendantly to be alive:
Though dim the word, oh, may you be
  Sublimed to Ecstasy.

424

GOOD IS ENOUGH

I have heard my old man say,
As he smoked in mellow mood:
"I opine that 'better' may
Be but the enemy of 'good'."
I think upon the way I trained
Thews of youth to steely bands
Till for life my heart I strained,
Walking on my silly hands.

Then again I've often writ
What I deemed was decent stuff;
Yet I've fiddled round with it,
Couldn't polish it enough.
Couldn't shape it to my mind,
Till I chucked it with a groan . . .
So it is, I often find,
Better to let well alone.

Now a moderate am I
Poets my perfection plan;
To be an average I try,
Just a gentle jingle man.
And though upon my lack I brood,
I have found by acid test:
Better be content with 'good',
Than break one's heart for 'best'.

INDIVIDUALIST

Because I am a self-made man
    And forged alone my fate,
I hate their molly-coddle plan
    Their Economic State.
From out the lowest of the low,
    Aye, from the very ditch,
I've traded bitter blow for blow,
    —And now I'm rich.

Because no man has aided me
    In all I've been and done,
In battle for security
    I owe not any one.
Let all upstand as I upstood,
    With hand and heart and mind;
Let each make good as I made good,
    —His level find.

Because I hate your Welfare State
    That breeds a weakling race,
I deem the days more truly great
    When brawn and brain had place;
When strong men strove to hold their own,
    And fought to win their way . . .
Social Security you prone,
    —The Hell, I say!

OLD SAM

Said Sam: "It don't sum up to sense
   That honest folk should arm and arm
And claim it's just in self-defence
   And none would do the other harm.
If no one's going to *attack*
   Why should we figger fighting back?"

"But anyway, it's daft to fight,
   Even for fatherland to fend;
Aye, though the cause be wrong or right
   War's just plain murder in the end.
And even in his country's need
   No lad should be compelled to bleed."

"And men of human conscience should
   Abolish frontiers everywhere;
And in the name of Brotherhood
   Of Nationality beware;
I thank the Lord that I am not,
   Said Sam, "a bloody patriot."

"Just let us have a common tongue,
   No barriers beneath the sun;
Freedom from fear for old and young,
   Their share of joy for everyone;
A common flag of faith unfurled,
   One hope, one dream, one race, ONE WORLD."

THE MILLENNIUM

We'll have no peace on this our earth
   If we persist in pride of birth;
If we believe our special race
   Above all others should have place;
Boasting: of peoples there are none
   To equal us beneath the sun.

Aye, though we flaunt a flaming flag
   Let us admit it's just a rag;
And humbly confess 'twould be good
   Could we abolish Nationhood.
We will go far to vanquish fear
   When we forget the word *frontier*.

When classes shall be levelled down
   And equal counted king and clown;
When rich and poor, four letters vain
   Are terms outworn of pride and pain;
And all religions equal stand,
   And each to each holds out the hand.

When we agree men crime intent
   Are victims of environment;
And yellow, brown and black and white
   Just human beings in God's sight;
When colour, creed and class combine
   To seek in man the source divine.

When strife of clan forever end
   And man to man be friend and friend;
When though we value fatherland
   It may for human freedom stand:
Then to the world at last will come
   Peace and the blest millennium.

CRUISE DE LUXE

Though bliss it be to grandly roam
   In foreign land or sea,
The joy of joys is coming home
   To domesticity.
And with content to settle down
   From travel wear and tear,
With slippers, pipe and dressing-gown
   In snug armchair.

When you have climbed the Pyramid,
   Admired the Taj Mahal,
Beheld a bull-fight in Madrid,
   Gondoled the Grand Canal,
How gleeful seems the garden patch
   With blooms of bonny hue!
How *Towser,* when you lift the latch,
   Leaps up at you!

You've drunk gin-slings in Singapore,
   Loafed in the *souks* of Fez,
Sun-bathed on Capri's silver shore,
   And scaled the heights of Eze.
For travel education is,
   And how you see and learn,
But, oh! the climax of your bliss
   Is your return!

Aye, though you comb the blasted earth
  And roam the seven seas,
But when beside the quiet hearth
  You cull your memories,
Then with the books and friends you love,
  You'll find in peace and rest
The end of travel is to prove
  That Home is best.

ANONYMOUS

When at the sign: Anthology
  I climb aboard a lyric bus,
The poems that appeal to me
  Are often by *Anonymous.*
Behold amid the classic crew
  Is one of whom Fame made no fuss,
A rhyming rascal no one knew,—
            Anonymous.

My name's a dud: 'mid poets I'm
  A leek among asparagus;
Yet let me make a lilt of rhyme
  And publish it anonymous;
Sweet, simple, short, a snatch of song
  Anthologists might prize, and thus
My lyric life I might prolong,—
            Anonymous.

So when senile and all forgot
  My memory is minimus,
In some anthology new-bought
  I'll read a rhyme anonymous:
A saucy air that pleaseth me,
  And I will say: "Who is this cuss?"
And wonder: "Are you he or she,—
            Anonymous?"

A VERSEMAN'S PLEA

If I should ever wax poetic
Please let me be apologetic;
For every verseman by mistake
A bit of poetry may make;
And sometimes it is really hard
Not to become a half-baked bard.

For stubbornly I dare to say
Pretentious poets of today
Are versemen ninety-five per cent;
And if censoriously bent,
You score out verse with pencil deft
You'll find there's mighty little left.

Yes, you may even play this game
With laureates of classic fame,
For those you designate divine
Have printed many a prosy line . . .
What, then, you may demand of me
Do *you* consider Poetry?

Originality of phrase,
Imaginatively ablaze;
The word unique, the magic fire,
That haunt, illumine and inspire;
Not lyric lilt, nor rhyme precision,
Not thought, not melody,—just VISION.

433

So in most poems, to my mind,
Ninety per cent of verse you'll find;
Cull out the pure poetic strains
And mostly vulgar verse remains.
—Well, better verse of worthy weight
Than poems less than second-rate.

TODAYS

Since every dawn may be my last
I've ceased to ponder on the past,
               Nor future plan;
As placid as a clovered cow
I'm living in the Here and Now,
               A happy man.

So honey-sweet, serene and gay
I seek to pattern each new day,
               Nor backward look;
And thus from out the passing page
I make, today, in my old age
               A radiant book.

'Tis thankful I'm to be alive.
(Would you not, too, at eighty-five?)
               And so I praise
The Present like a school-free boy
And squeeze the final juice of joy
               From my Todays.
Let each one be to me a gem,
And let me treasure all of them
               With rapture rare:
With gratitude for every one,
With song at sighting of the sun
               With eve a prayer.

SMALL VOICES

Because I writ myself to please,
I choose such simple themes as these,
As children, birds and brooks and trees.

Although for Love and Liberty
And Justice I would proudly plea,
Life's lowly things mean more to me.

O that I had Miltonic might
Could, like to Keats, beam starry light
Or soar with Shelley skylark height.

Alas! I have a common mind,
And meshed to meet the daily grind,
To earthiness am sore inclined.

And so in lilts of twos and threes
I make such rigmaroles as these,
Of children, birds and brooks and trees.

MY HOME

My home is like a citadel
        Of hushful hold;
Wherein with peace I deem to dwell
        Till I be cold;
A chubby chair, a friendly fire
        My last desire.

Four fondling walls with crinkled hands
        How I caress!
Blind to the lure of jewelled lands
        Here's happiness:
No more have I the heart to roam,—
        Just give me Home.

Far from the clangour and the strife
        I hug me in.
Here is the kindly close of life
        I've fought to win.
My lillied bastion of defence
        Ere I go hence.

Behold the quiet of my quest
        From wandering;
To hear in reverie of rest
        The kettle sing:
A kitten purring on my knee,—
        And toast,—and tea . . .

437

INGRATITUDE

So much have I forgot that makes
          Mischief of mind,
War, ruin and the tragic aches
          That rack mankind.
Yet strangely it's the little things
          Of long ago,
That rouse in me rememberings
          To work me woe.

Thoughts of the dear ones I have lost
          Whose love was vain;
How sadly now I pay the cost
          With grief and pain!
How wish them back that they might know
          With gentle cheer,
The tenderness I failed to show
          When they were near!

Are we not guilty, more or less,
          By word or deed,
Of lack of love, and carelessness
          To those in need?
And if to Heaven we would win
          In contrite mood,
Let us repent that bitter sin,
          INGRATITUDE.

PROUD EVENT

Alas! I know I have no hope
To celebrate my hundredth year,
For my poor heart will never cope
With fifteen winters more I fear;
But please, God, date my boneyard bedding
After I hold my Golden Wedding.

In June of nineteen sixty-three
Will dawn for me that happy day;
I guess that I'll be daft with glee,
With ninety just six months away.
And though Doc says I didn't oughter
I'll sluice my hatch with bubbly water.

The part of old grand-pa with pride
I'll play from overstuffed armchair,
While sitting pretty by my side
Is Granny of the silver hair;
And family fold:—my sole regretting
No *great* grandchildren grace the setting.

Heigh ho! It's fine at eighty-five
With happy heart to still survive;
To walk among my fellow men
And ply, I hope, a praiseful pen;
But how to God I'll be beholden
When I shall win to Wedding Golden!

THE SOURCE

I think the best work God has done
Was to create the blessed Sun;
I reckon it is better than
The sorry job he made of Man.
Compared with plain and peak and sea
What puny specimens are we.

So if of gods we must have one,
Why not let it be our Sun?
And let us worship day and night
The golden source of our delight;
Without whom we would not have birth
Nor any life would be on earth.

Between Dame Nature and old Sol,
And bird and beast and fish and all,
We do not matter very much;
And while I have the rhyming touch,
Let sun-glow on the grateful sod
Confirm, for me, my sense of God.

FEAR

Some say the spur is Fame
  That shapes a man's career;
But I believe his aim is fortified by Fear.
'Twas dread of dark unknown
  That made the savage raise
His gods of wood and stone
  And sing their praise.

So even to this day
  Fear fosters holihood;
Proud people crowd and pray
  In penitential mood;
Of virtue 'tis the drive,
Of honesty the source;
To every man alive
  A vital force.

It lurks behind the might
  And thunder of grim guns;
It fires us in the fight
  For wife and little ones;
It governs us for good,
  It fends us from defeat;
With safety for its mood
  Fear can be sweet.

Not all of us are brave;
   Life is a battle-field.
From cradle to the grave
   Let prudence be our shield.
Its power let us admit,
   Its glory chant and cheer,
Our saviour from the Pit,—
   Almighty FEAR.

CELLAR SONG

My dusty bottles row on row
I view with joy unceasing,
For prisoned in them dreams, I know,
Await divine releasing.
Château Lafite! I'll open it
And quaff a gay libation
To all who have the grace and wit
To drink in moderation.

A fig for preachers who persuade
That wine is of the devil!
Would Christ from water it have made,
If He had deemed it evil?
So here's to bottles row on row,
With silver cobwebs sheathing,
Their golden or their garnet glow,
To mirth bequeathing.

For God has made the vine to grow,
And willed the grape's fermenting;
And as his gift he doth bestow
I take it with contenting.
Ruby or amber be the cup,
So jovially given,
With reverence I raise it up,
Salute the Host of Heaven!

SOURDOUGH'S LAMENT

When I was a Klondike high-roller
  I tilted my poke with the best,
Though climate at times might be polar,
  I'd plenty of hair on my chest.
Now while I've no trace of rheumatics,
  And maybe I shouldn't complain,
I'm worried because I just ain't what I was,
  And I wish I was Eighty again.

I still have my love for the ladies,
  Chuck grand-mammies under the chin;
Yet, having a horror of Hades
  I'm kindo' allergic to sin.
Aye, though the hooch-bird be a-singing,
  I'm deaf to its dulcet refrain;
When the going gets rude you've gotta be good,—
  Gee! I wish I was Eighty again.

Some claim that the Nineties were naughty,
  Them statements I grieve to reverse;
You've got to be humble—not haughty
  To jiggetty-jog of the hearse.
I blink at the blonde in bikini,
  I shrink from the wink of champagne . . .
But *reforming,* by heck! What a pain in the neck!
  Gosh! I wish I was Eighty again!

444

OUR SAVING VICES

Virtue may be a form of Vice
   And Vice a phase of Virtue;
For indiscretion pay the price,
   As long as it don't hurt you
Just sow a crop of little sins,
   And husband them intently,
So that when old of age begins,
       You drop them gently.

Of course I mean a mild excess
   In eating or in drinking;
And love of ladies, more or less,
   Is tonic to my thinking.
Weakness may be a guise of strength,
   So in a senile crisis,
'Twill add to your existence length
       To shed some vices.

It is not good to be too good;
   Better to be just human.
Do not disdain delicious food,
   Fine wine or wile of women
And so, although the Kirk be stern,
   God may be more forgiving . . .
It takes a lot of life to learn
       The Art of Living.

THE TRAMP

"Lady," he said, "as lone you wait
                    By Convent Cross,
In youth you must have known a mate,
                    And mourned his loss.
A widow wan you may have been,
                    And shed sad tears;
But me,—my wife I have not seen
                    For fifty years.

"We quarrelled by the bridal bed;
                    She bade me go;
And if she be alive or dead
                    I do not know.
Nay, if she sat as you do now,
                    This Cross before,
I could not pick her out, I vow,
                    From fifty more."

Forlorn he scanned with wistful eye
                    That Sister grey;
Then, rising with a weary sigh,
                    He went his way.
Gravely she let him go,—she shed
                    No tardy tears,
For him to whom *she had been wed*
                    For fifty years.

THE OVERCOAT

Said Jane: "I found this scented note
In pocket of that old raincoat
        You hung to dry.
It seems to be a *billet doux,*
And reads: 'My heart is ever true,
        Your loving Vi'.
So I must ask you to explain,"
        Said Jane.

Said John: " 'Tis not for me, I swear.
Some joker must have put it there;
        I know no one
Who'd write to me: 'My dearest dear',
Although I must admit it's queer
        And far from fun;
With dame I've never carried on,"
        Said John.

Then as they tiffed with testy tone,
A ring upon the telephone
        Sudden was come.
Jane rushed to it: "It's your pal, Jim . . .
Hello! He's here,—I'm calling him . . .
        What's that? By gum!
I'll tell him . . . John for goodness sake,—
Last night you took home by mistake
        Jim's mackintosh!"

447

HUSBANDS

Some husbands are a sorry lot
  (Of course *you* are not one)
Who stop at bars and act the sot
  And come home with a bun;
Some play the ponies, pledge their pay,
  And stint their weary wives;
While some chase after blondes and may
  Lead double lives.

Though some men avaricious are,
  While some choleric be,
I deem the worst default by far
  Is *mental* cruelty.
A criticism harshly tuned,
  Let careless husbands know,
A gentle woman's heart can wound
  More than a blow.

The sadic mate who sulks apart,
  And fails to praise and bless,
Goes far to break a woman's heart
  In life's togetherness.
Than loud and brutish language worse,
  Or evil jealousy,
In wedded life the greatest curse
  Is Mental Cruelty.

OUR BOSSES

The power behind the race called human
I dare to deem is mostly Woman.
'Tis she who pulls the puppet strings,
Of pimps and parsons, clowns and kings.
By woman's wiles we men are swayed,
Bewitched, befuddled and betrayed.

Just scan the page of History,
And in its texture you will see
Key parts in the dramatic scene
Are played by courtesan and queen;
The while men brawl with brutal arms
The women win with wanton charms.

So may we males of modest mien
Who lumber the domestic scene,
Let wives with eloquence of jaw,
And lily hands lay down the law.
Behold I greet with heart of grace
Woman, the glory of the race
An all-wise God made man to vex
From Adam's rib—the Super Sex.

MATRONS

Forty's an age you dames don't like;
   You want to stall at thirty-nine;
And yet the bell of Time will strike,
   And every Mom must toe the line.
With aid of powder and of paint
   You cling to youth,—which ain't.

Alas! Your brats will soon grow up,
   Your teenage girls with lipstick toy.
Maturity's a bitter cup,
   Though beauty-parlours you employ;
You'd eat your cake and have it too,
   But—years will claim their due.

So when some tot says: "Grandma", though
   At first it gives you quite a shock,
Accept the part with pow of snow,
   And don't attempt to turn the clock.
At fifty don't for favours fish
   By claiming that you're *fortyish*.

Don't posture like a painted hag
   With golden locks at sixty plus:
Don't doll up like a gaudy rag
   And make yourself ridiculous . . .
Although at this, my rhyme, you rage,
   For godsake be your age!

450

BRATS

Said Miss McSniffie unto me:
    "Small children make me sore.
I think they are, you must agree,
    A veritable bore."
Said I: "If I subscribe to that
    Don't think me tart of tongue;
For what a nasty little brat
    You must have been when young."

Said Major Grumpy: "Kids be blowed.
    I can't stand them at all.
I think time would be well bestowed
    To wring their necks when small."
Said I: "Your sentiments may stink,
    And yet your mug assures
Me of their justice, and I think:
    Why didn't they wring *yours?*"

So all sour-pussies give you heed,
    Should children irk at play,
Doubtless, when young, you too had need
    Of patience more than they.
Yea, let us learn, e'er we go hence
    To mix with common dust,
The beauty of child innocence,
    The pathos of child trust.

THE MANAGING B——

Said Sam: "My wife, Jane has a jawbone that brays;
    She nags me from morning to night.
Whatever I does and whatever I says,
    She always is sure she is right.
She borrows my razor her bunions to cut;
    I'm scared that my pants she will snitch;
My wife is a wonderful house-keeper but—
    By gosh! she's a Managing Bitch.

Of course that's a word I never should use,
    So let me say: "Managing Blank".
And often I think as I'm shining her shoes,
    For her I've my mercies to thank.
It's true I am only a silly old mutt,
    And deem as I'm making her tea,
My missis is perfectly marvellous but—
    Must she be a Managing B——?

"I mustn't say this and I mustn't do that"
    She's telling me ten times a day.
It's true that I'm skinny and she's rather fat,
    But maybe it's better that way.
I do what I'm told, like a good little boy,
    The house runs with never a hitch . . .
But, O pals! I hope you will never enjoy
    A wife that's a Managing Bitch!

452

SMELL

Though my senses serve me well,
For delicacy, give me Smell.

The perfume of a bank of thyme,
Milk-heavy kine at homing time;
The burn of brush in Autumn air,
Green pippins piled for Winter care;
The tang of wrack at low of tide,
Blythe new-mown hay on meadow side.

Crisp bacon on the blaze to fry,
Old ale in tankard foaming high;
Aroma sweet of baking bread,
Rich onion soup for supper spread;
Roast beans of coffee, newly ground,
A morning kipper, buttered, browned.

The perfume of a silken slip,
The salty odour of a ship;
Morocco leather, Harris tweed,
The acrid air of stabled steed;
The pungency of paint and tar,
The fragrance of a fine cigar.

A piny wood, a clover lea,
A hawthorn hedge, a rosary;
A clump of wallflower, dewy wet,
And frankincense and mignonette . . .
But sweeter than them all, I swear,
The scent of Shiela's shampooed hair.

BOOK-ENDS

My father never read a book
  In all his days,
Though at them he would often look
  With wistful gaze.
So when I bought two nymph book-ends
  Of porcelain,
Saying: "Books are your dearest friends,"
  I spoke in vain.

A Tennyson and Browning I
  Between them stood;
The old man looked at them in shy,
  Distrustful mood.
I fear he would have junked the two
  With no regrets;
But oh! how fond he seemed to view
  The statuettes.

"I guess what I like best," said he
  With touching tact,
Is pottery more than pot'ry,
  And that's a fact.
But though to me them rhyming guys
  Are not so hot,
Believe me, son, I sure do prize
  Them *noods* a lot."

And there are many, I'm afraid
  Of father's trends,
Who think that books are merely made
  To fill book-ends.

MY LADY LUCK

One said to me: "Some gift you've shown,
    But also you've had luck."
I answered: "Yes, I humbly own
    I might have come unstuck.
'Tis true I have a modest name,
    And may be reckoned rich,
And yet I fought for fickle fame
    And came up from the ditch.

"A feckless Highland chiel was I
    Who crossed the sea with cattle,
And hit each ruddy railway tie
    From 'Frisco to Seattle;
For bread I often begged a bite,
    And lousy bunks I knew,
But fortune beamed on me the night
    I shot down Dan McGrew.

"For Dan McGrew and Sam McGee
    Saved me from sordid strife;
And I am greatful to these two
    For sunshine in my life.
My turning point in luck I see
    Refulgently began
The night I roasted Sam McGee
    And perforated Dan."

SLEEP SOUNDLY, SON

They say the guy who dropped the bomb
   From Hiroshima's height
Was troubled by a conscience qualm,
   And could not sleep at night,
Deeming that he had slain, perhaps,
   A hundred thousand Japs.

Don't worry, pal. Just think if they
   Had got the missile first,
How Baltimore would be today
   A hetacomb accurst;
How Japs would gibber in their joy,
   Manhattan to destroy.

Sleep soundly, son; for surely you
   Have earned a Nation's thanks;
No need your deed to ever rue,—
   You saved a million Yanks:
God bless your bloody bombing for
   Maybe it's ended War.

EXPERIMENTALIST

God fertilised the primal slime
  The saurians to fill;
Then in the crucible of Time
  He saw them kill;
Till sickened of their strife, no doubt,
  He wiped them out.

God tried again,—From reptile shape,
  Perfection as His plan,
Through the gorilla and the ape
  He fashioned Man.
To stunted creature of the cave
  A soul He gave.

God said: "Now you will work my Will,
  Of destiny divine . . .
But *no!*—ye seek new ways to kill,
  Spawn of the swine.
Fools! Even as my faith ye flout
  I'll stamp you out!

459

BOOK FIVE

COSMIC CAROLS

FACTS

A lawyer fellow reckoned wise
   Once said to me: "With proof I deal;
What are not facts I figure lies
   Illusionary and unreal."
Well, to his legal sense, no doubt
   It is a proper point of view:
But I have failed to figure out
   That only what is proved is true.

So to the scientific mind
   The reasoning is much the same.
To beauty's glamour it is blind
   And gives a flower a Latin name:
The stuff of fantasy and dreams
   It qualifies as mental mist:
The world would wiser be, it deems,
   If Keats had been a scientist.

Well, write me down as one who sees
   The glory granted to my sight;
When loveliness so much may please
   Why try to analyse delight?
I do not seek to know the truth
   Since sweet deception satisfies:
To hell with facts and sober sooth,
   God make me drunk with lies!

THE PEACE MAKER

Brothers, if you know how to pray,
  And prove yourselves unproud of men,
Profane your putty knees today
  And praise the great god Hydrogen.
Worship the power that saves you from
  Dark doom,—bless the Atomic Bomb.

Dropped from blue innocence on high
  In wink of eye to devastate
A host, or in mid-ocean sky
  A hundred hulls obliterate;
Making of army and of fleet
  Menaces vain and obsolete

So pile your precious missiles high;
  With planes and plans to flash their flight;
Then furious foe you may defy,
  And hordes will tremble at your might;
Though doubtless others do the same
  Peace *may* be bought with *fear* of flame.

For who would dare death to invite,
  Turn splendid city to a tomb,
For carnage and defeat to fight
  When even victory means doom.
So, brothers, bless the H bomb for
  Its *threat* could end the hell of war.

464

ATOMS

Life's but illusion, I am told.
Our senses make the world we see;
With mind inept we have no hold
On ultimate reality.
A billion atoms may compose
                    A radiant rose.

This solid flesh we feel and know,
Atomic density designs;
It is a frame of flux and flow
Whose border has no rigid lines:
Atom meets atom in the clutch
                    Of hands that touch.

And we ourselves are generate
Of laws that baffle our control:
Yet though we are the fools of fate
I hold in what I call my soul;
A hope, a faith, a light, a joy
                    No logic can destroy.

Let me believe that all I see,
(The sterile scientist despite),
Just as it is, was meant for me,
To win my wonder and delight . . .
A kiss: a childish hand to close:
                    The rapture of a rose!

MOON SONG

The sky is like a vasty cup
Of violet, and staring up,
Plumb in the middle like a spoon
Of silver I behold the moon.
It looks so cute, so cool, so calm,
As if it did not care a damn
For human worms the likes of us,—
I really don't suppose it does.

"Alas, poor man!" it seems to say;
"Alack, the hapless human race!
Frail creatures of an empty day,
Who come and go and leave no trace!
I knew your world before you were;
I'll know it when you cease to be;
And by my scorn you may infer
My sense of your futility."

Then to the moon I made reply:
"Of course I see your point of view.
Just now you dominate the sky,
But one day we'll be boss of you.
We scan you through a mighty glass,
Of your geography, recorders,
And one day it will come to pass
We'll run excursions to your borders.

"Yes, Mister Moon, you've got us right,
And yet I think you will agree,
Our transitoriness despite,
That clever little brutes are we.
We may be vapid, vague and vain;
Our species may be doomed to cease . . .
Yet, Moon, salute the human brain,
Creation's masterpiece!

EARTH SONG

A famous scientific guy
Who looks like a fantastic rabbit,
Has got me so bamboozled I
Resemble a bewildered Babbitt.
For half my life my bean I've strained
To solve the secret of Creation;
And now he's got it all explained
And packed up in a snug equation.

Of course I cannot understand
His cryptic hash of dash and bracket;
His figures and his fractions and
His symbols make a puzzle packet.
But wise men wag their beards and say:
"He must be right,—the man's a wizard,
And what we can't digest today,
In twenty years will suit our gizzard."

He looks an esoteric elf,
But, oh! one hopefully supposes
He understands it all himself,
Not thumbed his philosophic nose is?
He smugly sums the cosmic whole
With algebraic acrobatics . . .
That all is abstract and the sole
Reality is mathematics.

468

Of course I know the chap's an ace,
But how it robs life of elation
To see the joys of time and space
Confined within a curt equation.
To think all ecstasies that be
Can to a formula be shrunken . . .
Oh, hell! Reality to me
Is beer,—let me get drunken!

ASPIRATION

This brain-box, with its thirty million cells,
(Or more or less,—I really do not know),
That registers experience and swells
With wisdom, growing as we grow,
Coordinating personality,—
A tiny shock,—and it has ceased to be.

A tiny knock and all we know as "we",
The ardour of our eloquence and flame,
Forever and forever ends to be,
Goes back into the dark from which it came . . .
O ye proud peoples! grovel in the dust
From which you rose,—return to it you must.

Return you must, and pay the debt you owe
To Nature, while this brain miraculous,
This wealth of thirty million cells or so,
Will not be worth a lousy tinker's cuss
When you surrender it to Nature's claim
Into the elements from which it came.

Matter is indestructible; nothing is lost.
There is no death, no end, just change and change;
Our individualities are tossed
Into oblivion, but by some strange
Sweet chemistry tomorrow we may be
Petal of rose, or wing of honey-bee . . .
O God of Nature, please make me a tree.

470

LOWBROW

Of Relativity and such
I fear I don't know much;
I've tried so hard to comprehend
Its theories, but in the end,
Although it leaves me feeling small
I'm vague about it all.

Yet here I candidly avow
I'm glad I am not high of brow,
And I can say in sober truth
I don't believe in *too much* truth:
If you told me the world was flat . . .
I'd let it go at that.

But granted Spatial Time is true,
I ask myself what can it do
For common folk like you and me
Who make up most humanity?
If Man it cannot benefit
I have no use for it.

But is it not a grief to see
A grizzled grandfather like me
Who gags at Relativity?
When told by men whose brains are bright:
"Indubitably, Einstein's right!"
Just yawns and answers: "Quite."

WISE FOOL

It is not good with naked eye
Reality to see too nigh,—
   Best be half blind.
It is not well to strain the ear,
The music of the stars to hear,
   And discord find.
It is not wise to be too wise:
In knowledge disillusion lies,—
   Yea, I'm a fool;
But I would rather be a clown
Than college don in cap and gown,
   And campus rule.

Philosopher, with furrowed brow,
Far happier am I than thou,
   I dare to think.
My mind ferments no evil brew;
The dregs of Freud and Jung I do
   Not care to drink.
Professor, if you're asking me
What Relativity may be,
   My lips are dumb;
For theologians no brief
I hold, but hug a fond belief
   In Kingdom Come.

And having such a simple mind,
To take things as they are, I find
   Contentment brings.
So as my humble way I go
I do not know or seek to know
   The source of things.
For my philosophy is this:
A lassie's lips were made to kiss,
   Red wine to drink:
So let's be merry while we may:
'Tis better far to sing and play
   Than think and think
      And think.

H_2O

Chemists call water H_2O—
They may be right, I wouldn't know.
Of flowers and trees and singing birds
I cannot tell the Latin words.
For scientific sense, alas!
Just write me down a silly ass.

But Water Worshipper am I,
And will be to the day I die;
For when I was a barefoot boy
The swimming hole I sought with joy;
And now in age with limber glee
I leap into the lilac sea.

For Water to my wistful sight
Is rich refreshment and delight;
Clear claret in a lillied pool,
Or foamy white like carded wool;
And mist and steam and ice and snow
Are fancy forms of H_2O.

So thank God for the element
That health and joy to me has meant!
May crystal water to the end
Prove my profound and precious friend!
Let others to the dram-shop go,
I'll get me drunk on H_2O.

474

DECADENCE

The Prince, they say, has had his day
        And it was proud and high;
And now you meet him in the street
        On foot as you and I.
And though you note his shabby coat,
        A monocle he sports,
And has the flair so *débonnaire*
        Of protocols and courts.

The Prince is lean, his lips are green,
        His face is putty grey;
A meal of meat he cannot eat
        Because he cannot pay.
From Savile Row of long ago
        A threadbare suit he wears,
Yet as I pass he cocks his glass
        And stonily he stares.

But yesterday upon my way
        His haughtiness I met,
And such his glance of arrogance
        I dropped my cigarette,
For very shy and meek am I,
        Yet as I turned around
I saw him quick bend down and pick
        My fag from off the ground.

And so this morn I braved his scorn
      As in the sun we strolled;
A mild gold-flake I begged him take
      From out my case of gold.
Sour as a quince I saw him wince,
      His eye-glass he produced.
"No thanks" said he; "Hum! pardon me—
      Have we been introduced?"

L'ENVOI

I guess this is the final score;
Alas! I now shall write no more,
    Though sad's my mood;
Since I've been sixty years a bard,
I must admit it's rather hard
    To quit for good.

For three-score years I've roped in rhyme,
Till weary of the worn-out chime
    I've sought for new;
But I've decided in the end,
With thirty-thousand couplets penned,
    The old must do.

So let this be the last of me;
No more my personality
    I'll plant in verse;
Within a year I may be dead,
Then if my books are no more read,
    I'm none the worse.

Far better scribes than I have gone
The way to bleak oblivion
    With none to sigh;
Ah, well! My writing's been such fun,
And now my job of work is done,
Dear friends, who've let me have my run,
    Good-bye,—good-bye!